P9-CMF-739

Ideas C + W. had in common?
contributed to Lyrical Ballad
part of meter in poetry?
C.'s def. of poetry

# THE BEGINNINGS

## OF THE

# ENGLISH ROMANTIC MOVEMENT

## A STUDY IN EIGHTEENTH CENTURY LITERATURE

BY

### WILLIAM LYON PHELPS

A.M. (HARVARD), PH.D. (YALE)

LAMPSON PROFESSOR OF ENGLISH LITERATURE AT YALE COLLEGE

## GINN & COMPANY

BOSTON · NEW YORK · CHICAGO · LONDON

8 21.09
P54b

COPYRIGHT, 1893,
By WILLIAM LYON PHELPS.

ALL RIGHTS RESERVED.

66.1

The Athenæum Press

GINN & COMPANY · PRO-
PRIETORS · BOSTON · U.S.A.

TO

PROFESSOR J. P. MAHAFFY

OF TRINITY COLLEGE, DUBLIN, IN REMEMBRANCE

OF A FEW DAYS IN A DULL VACATION

MADE BRIGHT BY HIS

KINDNESS

# PREFACE.

———◦◦◦———

THIS little book gives the results of a search in English literature from 1700 to 1765, for the beginnings of the English Romantic movement. The minor poetry from 1725 to 1765, although desperately dull reading, has satisfactorily rewarded my search. I have reached no startling conclusions, but there is some matter in the book that may fairly be called new; and a number of points suggested by previous study have been more fully developed. The Spenserian Revival is treated with some approach to thoroughness, and my list of imitations I believe to be much longer than any other ever printed. In the discussion of Ballad Literature and in the chapter on Gray I have also gone carefully into details.

So far as I am aware no book has ever been written on the history of English Romanticism, so that the matter given here is the result of first-hand study. Every statement of fact and every critical opinion, unless the contrary is distinctly stated, are based on references to the original sources, so far as these have been accessible. The prose and poetry of the period I have read very largely in first and early editions. An original edition with the author's first preface is often of the greatest value to the student of a literary development.

The utmost care has been taken to secure accuracy in dates. In this kind of work dates are exceedingly important, and different histories, encylopædias and dictionaries vary so widely from each other, that accuracy is not always easy. Every doubtful date has here been followed up carefully, and the date finally given is based on the best evidences and authorities.

Duplicate copy ordered
2250  9 April '41
MJH.

In this book I have tried to establish two things. First, that the spirit of Romanticism has never been wholly extinct in English literature. Second, that between the years 1725 and 1765 the Romantic movement was a real, if quiet force, and that in these forty years may be found the seeds which sprang to full maturity in Scott and Byron, and in all the subsequent Romantic literature of the nineteenth century.

My thanks are due to the officials of the Boston Public Library, and to the librarians of Harvard and Yale Universities, who have always shown me the utmost courtesy. I cannot sufficiently express my obligations to Professor H. A. Beers of Yale, and to Professor Barrett Wendell of Harvard. It was at the suggestion of the former that I first entered upon this line of study, and the generous loan of his own manuscript notes on the period has been an invaluable help. It was Professor Wendell who first suggested the idea of printing my results, a thought that had not previously occurred to me. He also read all of the first draft of my manuscript and made many useful suggestions. My thanks are due to Professor John M. Manly of Brown, who read and annotated my manuscript, and to Professor George Lyman Kittredge of Harvard, who assisted me materially in countless places with his wide learning and unfailing kindness. Mr. Thomas Sergeant Perry of Boston, and Professor T. R. Lounsbury, of Yale, also read extracts and helped me by many fruitful hints, and by much friendly counsel; and I should also like to express in common with so many other students my appreciation of the inspiration and general stimulus I have received from the kind words of Professor F. J. Child. No sincere student ever came into close contact with this Teacher without becoming both a better scholar and a better man.

Any corrections of errors, or suggestions, will be gratefully received and promptly acknowledged.

W. L. P.

Yale University, 10 March, 1893.

# CONTENTS.

## CONTENTS.

# INTRODUCTION.

---

## WHAT IS ROMANTICISM?

ANY attempt to make a definition of Romanticism that will be at once specific and adequate is sure to result in failure. It is not simply that the word "Romantic" has both a popular and a critical sense, each of which differs widely from the other; but that the word is used *critically* in very different ways. For example, we say that Scott's counts are Classic, as distinguished from those of Keats, which are Romantic; but, speaking critically, it will never do to say that Scott was a Classic poet, because he certainly stands as one of the most prominent figures in English Romanticism.

Again, we call Byron a Romantic poet, because his poetry expresses that sentimental melancholy and vague aspiration which characterize the Romantic mood; but if we take Romanticism to be what Heine says it is — the revival of the life and thought of the Middle Ages — we certainly cannot class Byron as a Romantic poet.

The word Romanticism is also often applied not to subject, but to method. Any poet, like Victor Hugo for example, who rebels against and ignores the rules of the Classicists, is thereby a Romantic poet. In this sense Wordsworth might be, and in fact is, called a Romanticist, although he differs completely from Scott on the one hand, and from Byron on the other. When three poets so utterly unlike as Scott, Byron, and Wordsworth are each and all ranked by various critics as belonging to the Romantic school of English literature, it is easy to see that the term must be used in widely different senses.

I have seen many people who thought they could define Romanticism off-hand; but I have never seen one who could actually do it when brought to the test. It may be profitable to rehearse a few of the definitions given by critics and men of letters, in order to show the difficulty of getting at something that will satisfy everybody. Heine says, "Was war aber die romantische Schule in Deutschland? Sie war nichts anders als die Wiedererweckung der Poesie des Mittelalters, wie sie sich in·dessen Liedern, Bild- und Bauwerken, in Kunst und Leben, manifestiert hatte. Die Poesie in allen diesen Gedichten des Mittelalters trägt einen bestimmten Charakter, wodurch sie sich von der Poesie der Griechen und Römer unterscheidet. In Betreff dieses Unterschieds nennen wir erstere die romantische und letztere die klassische Poesie."[1] Then Heine goes on to say that in *antique* art the plastic figures are identical with the thing represented, with the idea which the artist seeks to embody and communicate, whereas in *romantic* art all descriptions, as, for example, the wanderings of a knight, have always an allegorical significance. Classic art portrays the finite, Romantic art the infinite.

Madame de Staël follows much the same idea. She says, "Le nom de romantique a été introduit nouvellement en Allemagne, pour désigner la poésie . . . qui est née de la chevalerie et du christianisme. . . . On prend quelquefois le mot classique comme synonyme de perfection. Je m'en sers ici dans une autre acception, en considérant la poésie classique comme celle des anciens et la poésie romantique comme celle qui tient de quelque manière aux traditions chevaleresques." She also remarks on "l'imitation de l'une et l'inspiration de l'autre."[2]

These two definitions evidently refer mainly to the subject-matter — the kind of topics handled by Romantic writers. Other definitions refer more to the subjective side — to the Romantic mood. Mr. Pater says, "The essential classical

[1] Die Romantische Schule (Cotta edition), page 158.
[2] De l'Allemagne, Vol. I., Chap. XXX. (Stuttgart, 1830).

element is that quality of order in beauty. . . . It is the addition of strangeness to beauty that constitutes the Romantic character in art. . . . It is the addition of curiosity to the desire of beauty that constitutes the romantic temper. . . . The essential elements, then, of the Romantic spirit are curiosity and the love of beauty; and it is as the accidental effects of these qualities only that it seeks the middle age." [1]

Again, Dr. F. H. Hedge declares that the Romantic feeling has its origin in wonder and mystery. "It is the sense of something hidden, of imperfect revelation. . . . The peculiarity of the classic style is reserve, self-suppression of the writer. . . . The Romantic is self-reflecting. . . . To the Greeks the world was a fact, to us it is a problem. . . . Byron is simply and wholly Romantic, with no tincture of classicism in his nature or works." [2] Dr. Hedge gave the essence of Romanticism as Aspiration. Prof. Boyesen writes, "Romanticism is really on one side retrogressive, as it seeks to bring back the past, and on the other hand, progressive, as it seeks to break up the traditional order of things. . . . The conventional machinery of Romantic fiction; night, moonlight, dreams . . . Romantic poetry invariably deals with longing, . . . not a definite desire, but a dim, mysterious aspiration." [3]

Now for some definitions referring neither to mood nor to subject matter, but to method. Mr. Saintsbury lays down this dictum. "The terms classic and romantic apply to treatment not to subject, and the difference is that the treatment is classic when the idea is represented as directly and with as exact an adaptation of form as possible, while it is romantic when the idea is left to the reader's faculty of divination assisted only by suggestion and symbol." [4] Victor Hugo, in the preface to *Hernani* (1830) said, "Le Romantisme, tant de fois mal défini, n'est . . . que le libéralisme en littérature." Toreinx, in his

1 *Macmillan's Magazine*, Vol. XXXV.
2 *Atlantic Monthly*, Vol. LVII.
3 Novalis and the Blue Flower, *Atlantic Monthly*, Dec., 1875.
4 A Short History of French Literature, page 582.

*Histoire du Romantisme en France*, says, " Les Romantiques sont ceux qui dans les arts veulent autre chose que ce qui est." M. Brunetière, in an exceedingly interesting article called *Classiques et Romantiques*,[1] says, " Le romantisme n'est pas n'importe quelle révolution, mais une révolution pour remettre en honneur tout ce que le classicisme avait, sinon dogmatiquement condamné, du moins effectivement rejeté. . . . Ils sont précisément aux deux poles de l'histoire de notre littérature nationale." Classicism he calls " la régularité du bon sens — la perfection dans la mesure," and Romanticism " le désordre de l'imagination — la fougue dans l'incorrection."

No one ever showed better the hopelessness of finding a satisfactory definition of Romanticism than Alfred de Musset, in his brilliant *Lettres de Dupuis et Cotonet* (1836). This correspondence is a charming burlesque. The two letter-writers try definition after definition, only to find that something extremely important has been left out, or that the definition is self-contradictory, or that it is ridiculously meaningless. They finally conclude that Romanticism consists in employing an abundance of glowing adjectives ; which, though meant to be laughable, is as helpful a definition as many that have been seriously urged.[2]

But, though all the above definitions of Romanticism make a confusing variety of opinions, we cannot help seeing that there is something in them common to all. Romantic literature will generally be found to show three qualities : Subjectivity, Love of the Picturesque, and a Reactionary Spirit. By the first quality I mean that the aspiration and vague longing of the writer will be manifest in his literary production ; by the second, that element of Strangeness added to beauty, which Mr. Pater declares is fundamental ; this may appear mildly, as where the writer is fond of ivy-mantled towers and moonlit

---

[1] *Revue des deux Mondes*, 15 Jan., 1883.

[2] Théophile Gautier's brilliant *Histoire du Romantisme* is full of interest ; and Mr. Courthope's last chapter in his *Life of Pope* has much that is pertinent and suggestive

water, or may turn into a passion for the unnatural and the horrible, as in tales of ghosts and of deeds of blood. And by the third is meant that the Romantic movement in any country will always be reactionary to what has immediately preceded; it may be gently and unconsciously reactionary, as in England, or proudly and fiercely rebellious, as in France.

Taking these three elements, Subjectivity, Picturesqueness, and Reaction, it is easy to see why the Romantic movement in England, in Germany, and in France, went for its inspiration back to the Middle Ages. Romanticism is certainly wider in connotation than Mediaevalism; and in the discussion of English Romanticism attempted in this book, the definitions of Heine and Madame de Staël would have to be supplemented and amplified to be adequate. But in the Middle Age lay just the material for which the Romantic spirit yearned. Its religious, military and social life and all forms of mediaeval art can hardly be better characterized than by the word *Picturesque;* and souls weary of form and finish, of "dead perfection," of "faultly faultless" monotony, naturally sought the opposite of all this in the literature and thought of the Middle Ages. And as the Classical Augustans had neglected this period above all others, and treated it with contempt, the Reactionists began with an attempt to revivify and brighten this forgotten Mediaeval life.

The most striking difference between the Romantic movement in France and in England is that in the former country the movement was *conscious*, while in the latter it was only *instinctive*. French Romanticism had a definite program, backed almost from the start by a brilliant critical school, headed by one supreme creative genius. English Romanticism was a totally different thing. Its beginnings are so faint and so far below the surface that many writers seem to believe that English Romanticism began with the nineteenth century, and that in the "age of prose and reason" there was no such thing as a Romantic movement at all. It is very true that the general character of eighteenth century literature was formal, critical, and prosaic; but it is also true that beneath this outward crust the fire of Romanticism was glowing. The volcanic eruption of genius which marked the first years of the present century can be explained only by the examination of previous conditions. These conditions I have endeavored to explain with some fullness and clearness; and the result ought to prove that the beginnings of the English Romantic movement should date back to the first quarter of the eighteenth century; and that during the second quarter, and especially during the fifth decade, the strength of the movement was much greater than seems to have been commonly supposed.

# CHAPTER I.

## PRINCIPAL LITERARY CHARACTERISTICS OF THE AUGUSTAN AGE.

THE literary characteristics of the so-called Classical or Augustan age of English literature are so well known, that I shall here discuss them only in a cursory manner. In tracing the early growth of the Romantic reaction, it is necessary to begin with a review of the prominent qualities of the Classical period; this may best be done by enumerating certain striking characteristics, and establishing these by examples taken directly from the literature of the time. We may proceed in the following order :

## I. THE VIEW OF LIFE. — THE ATTITUDE TOWARD RELIGIOUS AND PHILOSOPHICAL PROBLEMS.

As in every age, literature is simply the crystallization of tendencies of thought, so the Queen Anne school of English literature expressed the popular dominating ideas about the problems of life. Classicism was not merely a literary fashion, arbitrarily set by the leaders of taste; it had its roots deep in the prevailing religious and philosophical thought. The Augustan view of life was almost wholly *phenomenal*. A man like Addison carried his whiggism into everything. He resolutely closed his senses to feelings of Mystery and Awe; the idea of unseen and eternal realities, so constantly present to the Puritan mind, seems to have had no significance for men of his stamp. Respectability — decent Conformity — these were the watchwords of the Augustans. The view of life was equally unlike that of the Renaissance and of Puritanism.

In the former, boundless imagination, unspeakable aspiration, overflowing enthusiasm predominated; in the latter the vivid realization of the supersensual world, a religious creed full of the symbolism of Hebrew poetry, and a gloom that was as quickening to poetical and religious imagination as it was mortifying to earthly happiness. Now if there was anything the Augustans hated, it was Enthusiasm; they were simply bored by it, as the man of the world is bored by the naïve raptures of the unsophisticated. Those who naturally lacked enthusiasm abhorred the feeling; those who had it, cautiously and deliberately checked its expression as something childish and plebeian. On the religious side of popular belief, Mystery was hated and Respectability exalted. This was owing partly to a reaction against Puritanism, and partly to a skeptical indifference generated by the constant sectarian controversies of the seventeenth century. It was not simply fanaticism and intense religious zeal that were despised; the atheists, pronounced skeptics, and deists were hated with equal fervor, as men who were trying to unsettle and disturb the reign of respectable conformity. Mr. Ingersoll would have had no more influence over the typical Augustan than Mr. Moody. The fashion of conformity is curiously shown in the greatest man of the time, Swift. The Dean was as destitute of positive religious belief as can well be imagined; but the age forced him to masquerade as the most powerful champion of Christianity.

This view of life, with its absence of spontaneous enthusiasm and religious imagination, must never be forgotten in the study of the contemporary literature. I think that Pope, notwithstanding his manifest limitations, had more imagination and enthusiasm than he generally has credit for; but he was forced to bow to the public opinion which he himself had done so much to form. Mr. Leslie Stephen, in his admirable history of English thought, in comparing the relation between Milton, Spenser, and Pope, says that the first two could speak in a familiar symbolism; Pope had to take a creed of the time.

" But the thought had generated no concrete imagery. . . .
We have . . . diagrams, instead of pictures; a system of axioms
. . . instead of a rich mythology." [1]

## II. THE EXALTATION OF FORM OVER MATTER.

This was largely due to two causes: a reaction against the
" Metaphysical " school of poetry, and the following of French
models. The former has been well pointed out by Mr. Gosse
in his book *From Shakespeare to Pope*, although Mr. Gosse's
conclusions and assertions here as elsewhere must be taken
*cum grano salis*. By the beginning of the eighteenth century
the reaction against the school of Donne was complete. The
" surface " view of life disliked obscurity in literature as much
as mystery in religion. When Addison and his friends ridicule
" pointed antithesis," " forced wit," etc., they do not refer to
the pointed, antithetical style of Pope, but to the far-fetched
figures and subtile comparisons of Donne, Herbert, Crashaw,
and the rest. Pope's view of the Metaphysicals may be shown
most plainly by a letter to his friend Cromwell in 1710, on
the poet Crashaw. " All that regards design, form, fable, which
is the soul of poetry; all that concerns exactness, or consent
of parts, which is the body, will probably be wanting. Only
pretty conceptions, fine metaphors, glittering expressions, and
something of a neat cast of verse, which are properly the
dress, gems, or loose ornaments of poetry, may be found in
these verses. . . . No man can be a true poet, who writes
for diversion only. These authors should be considered as
versifiers and witty men, rather than as poets." [2] This last
phrase affords a particularly good example of the irony of fate,
because much modern criticism would use Pope's very words
in reference to himself; considering him as a versifier and
witty man rather than a poet. Indeed, not a few students

---

[1] *History of English Thought in the Eighteenth Century*, Vol. II., page 351, *et seq.*
[2] All my references to *Pope's Works* are to the Elwin-Courthope edition. The
present quotation is in Vol. VI., page 116.

of literature would call the author of *The Flaming Heart* a truer poet than the author of the *Essay on Man.*

French influence had also much to do with the formation of literary taste in England. Within the last few years there has been a movement among some critics which is an attempt to depreciate the influence of France on English literature — not only of the Augustan period, but also in the case of the Comic Drama of the Restoration. It is perhaps true that in the past, Gallic influence has been greatly exaggerated; but it is an element that cannot be overlooked. The Romanticists would not have rebelled against Voltaire and his countrymen so strongly, had the French influence been small; and French pressure on England was of course wholly in the direction of clearness and restraint. It reinforced the reaction against the Metaphysicals. Clearness was exalted above force, raiment above body, brilliancy above depth. The reason why Augustan literature is so transparently clear is not wholly due to the accuracy and care of the authors; it is owing largely to the subject matter. Men avoided difficult themes. Whether Pope and his friends pleased the English heart or not, they certainly suited the French. Voltaire always looked on Queen Anne literature as the high-water mark of English achievement. In 1760 he wrote in English to a British friend: "Though I do not like the monstrous irregularities of Shakespear; though I admire but some lively and masterly strokes in his performances, yet I am confident nobody in the world looks with a greater veneration on your good philosophers. You are now at the pitch of glory in regard to public affairs. But I know not wether you have preserved the reputation your island enjoyed in point of literature when Addison, Congreve, Pope, Swift were alive."[1]

---

[1] I transcribed this from the autograph letter in the British Museum.

## III. THE BELIEF THAT ALL TRUE LITERATURE CONSISTS IN FOLLOWING NATURE.

Nature is here used, of course, in a different sense from that in which we use the word when we speak of Thomson or Wordsworth as a follower of Nature. (The growth of nature-poetry was one of the strong tendencies in the Romantic movement, as will be pointed out later.) But the cry "Follow Nature" was the shibboleth of the Classicists. What they meant was an exact reproduction of every-day life and manners, as opposed to anything wild or extravagant, or that existed only in the writer's imagination. Nature meant with them little more than their deity, Common-Sense. Pope's *Essay on Criticism* sets forth the doctrine, and as Mr. Courthope has given so admirable an analysis of the *Essay*, I will quote him directly. "Three main principles underlie Pope's reasoning:

1. That all sound judgment and true 'wit' is founded on the observation of Nature;

2. That false 'wit' arises from a disregard of Nature and an excessive affection for the conceptions of the mind;

3. That the true standard for determining what is 'natural' in poetry is to be found in the best works of the ancients."[1]

This gives Augustan canons of criticism in a nutshell. The contemporary ideal of poetry appears again in a letter written by Lady Mary Wortley Montagu to Pope in 1717.[2] Speaking of the Iliad, she says Pope has passed it through his poetical crucible without its losing "aught of its original beauty." She calls Achilles "extremely absurd," and says she likes Ulysses, "who was an observer of men and manners" much better than "the hot-headed son of Peleus." This shows again what the Classicists meant by following Nature; it was not to describe the flowers and the trees and the changes of the seasons, or to use th language of common life — it was to copy the men and

---

[1] *Pope's Works*, Vol. V., page 49.   [2] *Ibid.*, Vol. IX., page 386.

manners of polite society — above all things to exclude what
was excessively emotional. Lady Mary's *Town Eclogues* were
good poetry, because they followed Nature; Joseph Warton'
*Enthusiast* did not follow Nature, being too subjective and
passionate.


IV. CLASSICISM.  IN WHAT SENSE WAS THE LITERATURE
       OF THE FIRST QUARTER OF THE EIGHTEENTH
       CENTURY CLASSICAL?

Here again we have a word most difficult to define because
it is used in so many different senses.  At this point it is
sufficient to repeat that the Augustan literature was not really
Classic; it was pseudo-classic.  As has often been said, it was
"more Latin than Greek, and more French than Latin."  It
lacked the element that gives to Greek literature its unpar-
alleled glory and charm — *Unconsciousness*.  The literature of
the school of Pope was painfully self-conscious; and here
we must remember that there is a great difference between
subjectivity and self-consciousness.  Romanticism is often
subjective, full of the passion and aspiration of the individual
composer; pseudo-classicism is self-conscious, in that the
author is constantly observing and laboriously polishing his
own workmanship.  He is like an opera singer ravished not
by the beauty of the aria or the dramatic passion of the scene,
but by the sound of her own voice.  But although the Queen
Anne literature lacked the Greek unconsciousness, it was
Classical in its clearness both of expression and of thought, in
the perfect adaptability of language to sense; it was Classical
in its repression of emotion, in its limited imagination; it
was Classical in its faithful obedience to critical rules, in its
suppression of individuality to the mandates of established
law; it was Classical in its intellectuality, and enthronement of
Reason.  As Professor Beers says,[1] "Its sole Latin master

[1] In an unpublished lecture.

was Horace," and "not Horace in his odes, but in his Epistles and Satires, and even then Horace as seen through the spectacles of Boileau." The Augustans were conscious Classicists; they thought it no shame to say they were imitators; their standard of excellence they clearly understood, and fidelity to the model was valued more than any spontaneity which diverged from it. We know how profoundly Pope was influenced by Walsh's words, written to him in 1706.[1] "The best of the modern poets in all languages are those that have the nearest copied the ancients."

## V. SUPREMACY OF TOWN OVER COUNTRY LIFE.

Dr. Johnson was simply carrying on Augustan ideas when he said that the best sight for a Scotchman's eyes was the road that led to London; and in all his love for the city and failure to appreciate natural scenery he was entirely in accord with the preceding age. It is true that Pastoral poetry flourished like the green bay-tree; but these compositions — with one exception to be noticed later — show even more clearly than the society satires, how utterly lacking the age was in appreciation of rural life. The Augustan Pastorals were artificial to the last degree, and form the best evidence that their authors had no first-hand knowledge of the scenes they attempted to portray. Their Pastorals were simply hollow imitations of classic models — Theocritus and Vergil. The literary monarchs had no genuine love for the country; the drawing-room, the theatre and the coffee-house absorbed all their attention. In their judgment, the country was no place for a healthy mind. It should be taken as medicine, not as diet. This view appears in a letter from Pope to Mrs. J. Cowper, written in 1722. "I . . . wish you may love the town . . . these many years. It is time enough to like, or affect to like, the country, when one is out of love with all but one's self."[2]

---

1 *Pope's Works*, Vol. VI., page 53.  2 *Ibid.*, Vol. IX., page 420.

## VI. THE FONDNESS FOR WIT, SATIRE AND TRAVESTY AS LITERARY SUBJECTS.

A large proportion of all the Queen Anne and early Georgian literature is composed of work wholly or in part satirical. This is seldom a sign of health, as it indicates that original composition and spontaneousness of imagination have succumbed to the reign of the critics. The cold, hard worldliness of Augustan life found its natural expression in polished wit and satire ; and the sarcasm was not directed against Sin, but against Dullness and Unconventionality — another bad sign. Many people wrote satires because they couldn't write anything else, not because they wished to lash any particular vice. Even Young and some of the Romanticists followed the popular taste and composed satires. The people were so deficient in natural emotion and higher imagination that the best men felt forced to yield to the prevailing demand — for the law of supply and demand affects the market of literature in much the same way as it fixes the price of wheat. In those days people wrote satirical pamphlets for the same reason that people to-day write sonnets for magazines. Pope, writing to Walsh in 1706,[1] said, " I have not attempted anything of a pastoral comedy, because I think the taste of our age will not relish a poem of that sort. People seek for what they call wit, on all subjects, and in all places ; not considering that nature loves truth so well, that it hardly ever admits of flourishing. Conceit is to nature what paint is to beauty." Matthew Arnold's remark that Gray would have been another man in a different age, would be much nearer the truth if spoken of Pope ; for the great wit and satirist did have occasional touches of emotion and imagination, which, in another age, he would have fostered rather than repressed. The brilliant and beautiful Lady Mary Wortley Montagu represents even better than

---

[1] *Pope's Works*, Vol. VI., page 51. This was the letter that called out Walsh's famous advice.

Pope and Addison the limitations of the Augustan days. With all her intellectual power, she does not seem to have been guilty of a single touch of real feeling or lofty imagination. The spirit of the age spoke out in her when she answered Pope's letter containing his verses on the country lovers struck by lightning; she replied by a coarse, doggerel burlesque.[1]

## VII. THE ATTITUDE TOWARD OLD ENGLISH WRITERS.

The rank and file of the Classicists regarded the old English writers not with absolute contempt, but with indifference. This indifference arose usually from ignorance. Shakspere was commonly regarded as the greatest English writer, although he was often handled in a way that would nowadays be thought sacrilegious; and even though admired, he was not very widely read and by no means always understood. Chaucer was not thought worthy of serious treatment, as is shown by Pope's disgusting Imitation. The people at large were grossly ignorant of him. Spenser fared not much better than Chaucer; those who knew him did not generally regard him as worthy of serious study; indeed it was by reviving Spenser that the Romanticists did some of their best work. Milton had been neglected, but only partially so; and his day was rapidly coming; he had, especially through his minor poems, a powerful influence on the Romantic movement.

Outside of these four great names, old English writers were buried in the dust-heaps of the past. The splendor and exuberance of the Elizabethan drama had been forgotten in the attention paid to the insipid, moralizing Augustan stage; the old dramatists were empty names. The old English style in poetry and romance was generally spoken of as "Gothic," a term of reproach, "synonymous with barbarous, lawless and tawdry." [2] Even Shakspere was half Gothic; if he was a great dramatist, he was no playwright; and he was full of excres-

---

[1] *Pope's Works*, Vol. IX., page 410.     [2] Prof. Beers's Unpublished Lectures.

cences.   True English poetry began with Waller.   To show
how roughly Shakspere was handled, let us look at one of
Dr. Atterbury's letters to Pope.   Atterbury, like Lady Mary,
was a genuine Augustan.   He writes in 1721, "I have found
time to read some parts of Shakespeare, which I was least
acquainted with.   I protest to you in a hundred places I cannot
construe him.   I do not understand him.   The hardest part of
Chaucer is more intelligible to me than some of those scenes,
not merely through the faults of the edition, but the obscurity
of the writer, for obscure he is, and a little (not a little) inclined
now and then to bombast, whatever apology you may have
contrived on that head for him.   There are allusions in him to
an hundred things, of which I know nothing and can guess
nothing. . . .   I protest Aeschylus does not want a comment
to me more than he does."[1]

Perhaps the extreme example of inability to appreciate
Shakspere is afforded by William Hamilton of Bangour,
(1704–1754), the author of the *Braes o' Yarrow*.   Hamilton
really liked Shakspere, but that did not prevent him from
"versifying" him.   He had the audacity to put Hamlet's
soliloquy into the heroic couplet, and he meant it all seriously:

> "My anxious soul is tore with doubtful strife,
>     And hangs suspended betwixt death and life ;
>     Life ! death ! dread objects of mankind's debate !
>     Whether superior to the shocks of fate,
>     To bear its fiercest ills with steadfast mind,
>     To Nature's order piously resign'd,
>     Or, with magnanimous and brave disdain,
>     Return her back th' injurious gift again."[2]

He also put part of King Lear into the couplet, with equal
success.[3]

[1] *Pope's Works*, Vol. IX., page 26.   This is the celebrated divine and Bishop of
Rochester, Francis Atterbury (1662–1732).   He was very intimate with Augustan
men of letters, especially Pope and Swift.
[2] Hamilton's *Poems and Songs*, page 65.
[3] *Ibid.*, page 172.

Another interesting bit of Augustan appreciation of Shakspere is found in David Mallet's poem, *Of Verbal Criticism.* For an example of infelicitous discrimination, it is worth reading:—

> "Great above rule and imitating none ;
> Rich without borrowing, nature was his own ;
> Yet is his sense debas'd by gross allay :
> As gold in mines lies mix'd with dirt and clay.
> Now, eagle-wing'd, his heavenward flight he takes ;
> The big stage thunders, and the soul awakes ;
> Now, low on earth, a kindred reptile creeps ;
> Sad Hamlet quibbles, and the hearer sleeps."

Pope had to speak apologetically about Shakspere, as he did about other things that he admired, which were contrary to the public taste. His Preface to his edition of Shakspere goes just as far as he dared.[1]

How Milton was regarded even by the elect may be seen by another letter from Atterbury. He writes to Pope in 1722, about *Samson Agonistes.* This poem appealed to Atterbury not because it was Milton—rather in spite of that fact—but because it was Classical. He thinks that with Pope's improvements it will pass. "Some time or other, I wish you would review, and polish that piece. If upon a new perusal of it . . . you think as I do, that it is written in the very spirit of the ancients, it deserves your care, and is capable of being improved, with little trouble, into a perfect model and standard of tragic poetry."[2] No wonder the Wartons took every opportunity to bring Milton into popular recognition.[3]

---

[1] *Pope's Works*, Vol. X., page 534.
[2] *Ibid.*, Vol. IX., page 49.
[3] In the Preface to C. Gildon's *Art of Poetry* (1718) there is a good word spoken for Shakspere and Spenser.

## VIII.  THE ATTITUDE TOWARD ANYTHING SAVOURING OF ROMANTICISM.

Romantic literature could hardly hope to find favor in an age whose standard was one of fidelity to every-day life and exact copying of Franco-Latin models.  When the Augustans called a poem or story "romantic," they meant that it was either wildly improbable and extravagant or else over-sentimental; and in either case it deserved an unqualified condemnation.  Everything must conform to their own standard of criticism; otherwise, it could not hope for the serious consideration of sane men and women; and if there was anything on which the Augustans prided themselves, it was their perfect sanity — their immense superiority in reason and common-sense over their own ancestors and over the nations of the north and east.  Pope chafed a little under this rigid exclusion of Romanticism, for in his sentimental correspondence with Lady Mary, he writes in 1716, "The more I examine my own mind, the more romantic[1] I find myself. . . .  Let them say I am romantic; so is every one said to be that either admires a fine thing or praises one; it is no wonder such people are thought mad, for they are as much out of the way of common understanding as if they were mad, because they are in the right."[2]

Lady Mary hated Romanticism, but admired Theocritus; she therefore cannot have him included among the Romanticists.  She writes to Pope in 1717, "I no longer look upon Theocritus as a romantic writer; he has only given a plain image of the way of life amongst the peasants of his country, . . . I do not doubt, had he been born a Briton, but his *Idylliums* had been filled with descriptions of threshing and churning."[3]  Again, we have some more testimony against Romanticism from Dr. Atterbury.  Pope sent him some Arabian Tales, half-recommending them himself, and asking for Atterbury's opinion.

---

[1] Meaning sentimental.          [2] *Pope's Works*, Vol. IX., page 360.

[3] *Ibid.*, Vol. IX., page 374.

The latter replies : " And, now, Sir, for your Arabian Tales. . . . Indeed they do not please my taste ; they are writ with so romantic an air, and, allowing for the difference of eastern manners, are yet, upon any supposition that can be made, of so wild and absurd a contrivance (at least to my northern understanding), that I have not only no pleasure, but no patience, in perusing them. . . . They may furnish the mind with some new images, but I think the purchase is made at too great an expense." [1]

This gives a very good idea of the Augustan attitude toward Romanticism ; but the best case I have succeeded in finding occurs in a letter of Lady Mary's to Pope — the same letter quoted above in which she speaks of Theocritus. Lady Mary writes from Adrianople — she has come upon some Turkish verses and she gives them first in their literal form, and then puts them " into the style of English poetry," with what success will presently appear. Speaking of the Turks, she says, " They have what they call the *sublime*, that is, a style proper for poetry, and which is the exact Scripture style. . . . I have it in my power to satisfy your curiosity, by sending you a faithful copy of the verses that Ibrahim Pashá, the reigning favourite, has made for the young princess, his contracted wife. . . . The verses may be looked upon as a sample of their finest poetry ": —

### STANZA I.

1. " The nightingale now wanders in the vines ;
   Her passion is to seek roses.

2. I went down to admire the beauty of the vines ;
   The sweetness of your charms has ravish'd my soul.

3. Your eyes are black and lovely,
   But wild and disdainful as those of a stag."

[1] *Pope's Works*, Vol. IX., page 22. This letter was probably written in 1720.

### Stanza II.

1.  " The wish'd possession is delay'd from day to day ;
    The cruel Sultan Achmet will not permit me
    To see those cheeks, more vermilion than roses.

2.  I dare not snatch one of your kisses ;
    The sweetness of your charms has ravish'd my soul.

3.  Your eyes are black and lovely,
    But wild and disdainful as those of a stag."

### Stanza III.

1.  " The wretched Ibrahim sighs in these verses ;
    One dart from your eyes has pierc'd thro' my heart.

2.  Ah ! when will the hour of possession arrive ?
    Must I yet wait a long time ?
    The sweetness of your charms has ravish'd my soul.

3.  Ah ! Sultana ! stag-ey'd ! — an angel amongst angels !
    I desire, — and my desire remains unsatisfied. —
    Can you take delight to prey upon my heart ? "

### Stanza IV.

1.  " My cries pierce the heavens !
        My eyes are without sleep !
    Turn to me, Sultana — let me gaze on thy beauty.

2.  Adieu — I go down to the grave.
        If you call me — I return.
    My heart is hot as sulphur ; — sigh, and it will flame.

3.  Crown of my life ! fair light of my eyes !
        My Sultana ! my princess !
    I rub my face against the earth ; —
        I am drown'd in scalding tears — I rave !
    Have you no compassion ?   Will you not turn to look
        upon me ? "

Lady Mary then gives a general criticism and finally says, "What if I turned the whole into the style of English poetry, to see how it would look?"

She "versifies" it as follows : —

### STANZA I.

"Now Philomel renews her tender strain,
Indulging all the night her pleasing pain ;

I sought the groves to hear the wanton sing,
There saw a face more beauteous than the spring.

Your large stag-eyes, where thousand glories play,
As bright, as lively, but as wild as they."

### STANZA II.

"In vain I'm promis'd such a heav'nly prize ;
Ah ! cruel Sultan ! who delays't my joys !

While piercing dreams transfix my am'rous heart,
I dare not snatch one kiss to ease the smart.

Those eyes ! like, etc."

### STANZA III.

"Your wretched lover in these lines complains ;
From those dear beauties rise his killing pains.

When will the hour of wish'd-for bliss arrive?
Must I wait longer? — Can I wait and live?

Ah ! bright Sultana ! maid divinely fair !
Can you, unpitying, see the pains I bear?"

### STANZA IV.

"The heavens relenting, hear my piercing cries,
I loathe the light, and sleep forsakes my eyes ;
Turn thee, Sultana, ere thy lover dies.

> Sinking to earth, I sigh the last adieu ;
> Call me, my goddess, and my life renew.
>
> My queen ! my angel ! my fond heart's desire !
> I rave — my bosom burns with heav'nly fire !
> Pity that passion which thy charms inspire."

Lady Mary adds, "I cannot determine upon the whole how well I have succeeded in the translation, neither do I think our English proper to express such violence of passion, which is very seldom felt amongst us." This last clause is significant.

I have given this extract at length, because it shows so clearly the limitation of the Augustan mind. No reader of to-day would hesitate in answering the question as to which of these two versions was the more poetical. The fact that Lady Mary lays the blame of the short-comings of her translation on the English language, and not on her own uninspired couplets, is very suggestive. But she was not the only person who thought that the orthodox form of versification was necessary to poetry ; Hamilton's version of Hamlet's soliloquy is a case in point, and even in the latter half of the century, when the Romantic movement was a reality, Macpherson thought seriously of putting *Ossian* into the Heroic Couplet.

# CHAPTER II.

## REACTIONARY TENDENCIES DURING THE AUGUSTAN AGE.

In support of the proposition that the spirit of Romanticism has never been wholly extinct in English literature, it may be interesting to notice certain reactionary tendencies which were present even in the height of the classical period. Such writers as Samuel Croxall, Lady Winchelsea,[1] Thomas Parnell, Allan Ramsay, William Hamilton of Bangour, are not easy to classify; they can hardly be said to belong to the new Romantic movement, nor do they preserve the seventeenth century traditions of Romanticism. It is perhaps better to consider them as currents flowing in a direction opposite to the general stream; individualities who were really out of sympathy with the Augustans, but who were overpowered by the prevailing fashion — partly because the fashion was so strong, partly because no one of them had sufficient force publicly to throw off the shackles. But, though their light was under a bushel, they have a genuine significance to the student of a literary movement. They show that the reign of Classicism was not complete. Attention has already been called to the fact that even the monarch himself was not wholly satisfied with his reign. Pope's lines in Thomson's *Seasons* have a peculiar ring, when we know their authorship.[2] It is rather surprising that Pope should have assisted Thomson in any way, because the latter was one of the early and powerful forces in the Romantic

---

[1] Also spelled Winchilsea.

[2] The lines in *Autumn*, beginning

"Thoughtless of beauty, she was beauty's self."

Mr. Perry has some interesting remarks on this passage: see his *English Literature in the Eighteenth Century*, pages 386 and 387.

reaction, though certainly not always conscious of the fact.
But Pope himself did some work that in aim, at any rate, was
not wholly Augustan. *Windsor Forest*, in spite of Wordsworth's
complimentary allusion,[1] can hardly be said to be anything
more than artificial; in *Eloisa* and in the *Unfortunate Lady*,
however, amid much coldness and artificiality, we have occasional touches of genuine passion and pathos, which suggest
what Pope might have done had he wholly freed himself from
contemporary influences. A mystery surrounds the *Elegy* —
we do not know the circumstances by which it was conceived;
but the warmth of *Eloisa* may be largely explained on purely
personal grounds, which fact, of course, robs it of much of its
significance as an index to Pope's general taste in poetry. No
one who reads Pope's correspondence with Lady Mary can
avoid the conclusion that the poet embodied in this *Epistle*
much of his own sentimental longings; for Pope's attitude
toward the brilliant society woman was certainly more than
that of conventional gallantry. He himself realized that *Eloisa*
was different from the general nature of his literary production.
Writing to Mrs. Martha Blount in 1716, he says, "The Epistle
of Eloisa grows warm, and begins to have some breathings of
the heart in it, which may make posterity think I was in love." [2]
And in sending the poem to Lady Mary in 1717, he adds,
"You will find one passage, that I cannot tell whether to wish
you should understand, or not," [3] presumably referring to the
closing lines,

> "And sure if fate some future bard shall join" etc.[4]

But though Pope's nature and passion poetry can hardly be
said to show much distinct non-conformity with prevailing

---

[1] *Wordsworth's Prose Works*, Vol. II., page 118.

[2] *Pope's Works*, Vol. IX., page 264.

[3] *Ibid.*, Vol. IX., page 382.

[4] The original editor of the edition of Pope does not agree with this view that
*Eloisa* is largely the expression of personal feeling. See Note in Vol. IX., page 264.
Mr. Courthope, however, is in substantial agreement with the view expressed in these
pages. See Vol. V., page 135.

ideas, a few passages in his private correspondence show glimpses of Romantic feeling. He writes to Mrs. J. Cowper in 1723, "I could wish you tried something in the descriptive way on any subject you please, mixed with vision and moral ; like pieces of the old Provençal poets, which abound with fancy, and are the most amusing scenes in nature. . . . I have long had an inclination to tell a fairy tale, the more wild and exotic the better ; therefore a *vision*, which is confined to no rules of probability, will take in all the variety and luxuriancy of description you will ; provided there be an apparent moral to it. I think one or two of the Persian tales would have given one hints for such an invention." [1] This outbreak is very suggestive.

But although it is half paradoxical to speak of Romanticism in Pope, there was a quiet, retiring figure of the time whose poetry displays some tendencies wholly contrary to Augustan feeling. It is worth noticing that he was an intimate friend of Pope's, and that the latter first edited his works. I refer to Thomas Parnell (1679–1717).[2] It is not true, as Mr. Gosse says, that he "published nothing." [3] *The Hermit* was published in 1710, and he printed in miscellanies a number of pieces which Pope collected and published in 1722. Still it was largely owing to the influence of Pope and Swift, that he was brought out of his Ulster obscurity, and induced to exercise his poetic gifts. His best known piece, *The Hermit*, and his *Satires* are in the Classic style ; but certain other of his writings have a real significance in the history of Romanticism. Mr. Gosse remarks with much truth, " there lay unvisited a romantic island

1 *Works*, Vol. IX., page 431.

2 Considerable difference of opinion seems to prevail as to the date of Parnell's death. Dr. Johnson says he died in July, 1717. Goldsmith, in his *Life of Parnell*, gives the same date, but later on in the very same account, says "he died in the year 1718." Ryland's *Chronological Outlines* gives the date 1717. The Encyclopaedia Britannica (9th edition) says 1718. Mr. Gosse (in Ward's *English Poets*, Vol. III., page 132) says Parnell "was buried at Chester on the 18th of October, 1718."

3 *Eighteenth Century Literature*, page 137.

of poesy, which was his by birthright." [1]  His *Night-Piece on Death* is very interesting as the fore-runner of the grave-yard literature of Young, Blair, and the rest, and especially as the prototype of Gray's *Elegy.* Compare these lines from the *Night-Piece :* —

> " Those graves, with bending osier bound
>      That nameless heave the crumbled ground,"

with the well-known stanza from Gray.

But besides Parnell's significance as the first of the church-yard poets, there is in his poetry a genuine feeling for Nature, which is very unlike the Augustan spirit, and which even suggests Wordsworth. [2]  It seems as if the latter might have named Parnell along with Lady Winchelsea in his famous utterance in 1815.  These lines from the *Night-Piece* show real love of nature.  The poet forsakes the books of the schoolmen for the wisdom of the sky and stars : —

> " How deep yon azure dyes the sky !
>      Where orbs of gold unnumbered lie,
> While thro' their ranks in silver pride
>      The nether crescent seems to glide.
> The slumbering breeze forgets to breathe,
>      The lake is smooth and clear beneath,
> Where once again the spangled show
>      Descends to meet our eyes below."

Goldsmith preferred the *Night-Piece* to Gray's *Elegy;* but Dr. Johnson, although uniformly unjust to Gray, did not agree with his friend in this instance.

Parnell's *Hymn to Contentment* also shows true nature-feeling. The following passage seems especially to foreshadow Wordsworth : —

> " The sun that walks his airy way,
>      To light the world, and give the day;
> The moon that shines with borrowed light;
>      The stars that gild the gloomy night;

---

1 Ward's *English Poets*, Vol. III., page 133.
2 See Mr. Gosse's *Eighteenth Century Literature*, page 137.

> The seas that roll unnumbered waves ;
> The wood that spreads its shady leaves ;
> The field whose ears conceal the grain,
> The yellow treasure of the plain :
> All of these and all I see,
> Should be sung, and sung by me ;
> They speak their Maker as they can,
> But want and ask the tongue of man." [1]

It is worthy of note that both these poems of Parnell are in the octosyllabic couplet, a measure that he handled with singular grace and charm. This verse-form was one largely employed by the Romanticists.

Besides Parnell's nature poetry, and melancholy mood, he gives us a breath of real Romanticism in his *Fairy Tale*. It opens thus : —

> " In Britain's isle, and Arthur's days,
> When midnight fairies danced the maze,
> Lived Edwin of the Green ;
> Edwin, I wis, a gentle youth,
> Endowed with courage, sense and truth,
> Though badly shaped he been."

This is one of the first faint echoes of Mediaevalism.

Anne Finch, Countess of Winchelsea (died 1720), may also be considered among the reactionary tendencies of the age. She has attained some prominence in literary history, owing to Wordsworth's remark in 1815, alluded to above; but her poetry has been very little read, and is not at all easy to find. She was a friend of Pope's, and exchanged poems with him on *The Rape of the Lock*. Her lines to him —

> " Our admiration you command
> For all that's gone before ;
> What next we look for at your hand
> Can only raise it more " [2] —

---

[1] See also the quotation Mr. Gosse gives, *Eighteenth Century Literature*, page 137. Mr. Gosse is wrong, however, in saying, " The *Hymn* opens thus." He has taken a passage not from the beginning.

[2] *Poems by Eminent Ladies* (1755), Vol. II., page 314.

do not sound like the words of a rebel against the Augustan age; and, indeed, she was not. Mr. Gosse says: "She was entirely out of sympathy with her age, and her talent was hampered and suppressed by her conditions. She was the solitary writer of actively-developed romantic tastes between Marvell and Gray, and she was not strong enough to create an atmosphere for herself within the vacuum in which she languished."[1] These are the words of a charmingly inaccurate writer, and have every symptom of the fatal "enthusiasm of discovery." Mr. Gosse also remarks elsewhere: "It is impossible to say whether she was the last of the old, or the first of the new romantic school."[2] I should say she was neither, but in general feeling an Augustan, with an under-current of real love for nature. It is in her fondness for country life, her love of out-door beauty, and her accurate descriptions of nature, that she differs from her contemporaries. In these important points, she may certainly be classed as reactionary in tendency. Her octosyllabic ode, *To the Nightingale*, has true lyric quality, and her short poems, *The Tree* and *A Nocturnal Reverie*, are notable expressions of nature-worship.[3] The last named is in the heroic couplet.

An interesting figure of the time is Samuel Croxall (died 1752).[4] He is remembered to-day chiefly as the translator of Æsop's *Fables;* most of his original poetry has been forgotten. With the exception of one poem, to be noticed later, his effusions found little favor among his contemporaries. Croxall was celebrated more for his preaching than for his poetry. He seems to have been wholly out of sympathy with the spirit of the age, even consciously and defiantly so. His poetical master was Spenser, for whom he had a fervent admiration in a time when Spenser was comparatively neglected. His important contributions to the Spenserian revival

---

[1] *Gossip in a Library*, page 123.

[2] *Eighteenth Century Literature*, page 35.

[3] These three poems are in Ward's *English Poets*, Vol. III., pages 29–31.

[4] Date of his birth unknown; he died at a venerable age.

will be discussed later ; but the first work of his that concerns our present purpose is *The Vision,* published in 1715. This is in the heroic couplet, but the style of the poem is distinctly unorthodox. It describes a vision of the ancient kings and queens of England, and the opening pictures of the woods and flowers and streams have a perceptible Romantic coloring. Besides the crowned heads, the poet has a vision of two English poets, not Cowley and Waller, but, strange to say, Chaucer and Spenser. He thus describes them : —

> " Chaucer the Parent of Britannic Lays
> His Brow begirt with everlasting Bays,
> All in a Kirtle of green silk array'd
> With gleeful smile his merry Lesson play'd.
> His fellow Bard beside him Spenser sate
> And twitch'd the sounding Chords in solemn State:
> An Ivy Garland on his Temples hoar
> With Sprigs of Laurel interwove he wore.
> Adown his Shoulders hung a Mantle blue
> Bedrop'd with Spangles of a Golden Hue ;
> Of Arms and Elfin Knights he mus'd his Song,
> And taught in Mystic Tales the list'ning Throng."

It is disappointing to find at the conclusion of this poem, that the work has a theological purpose — to attack Popery ; but even this unfortunate ending does not rob the poetry of its rich and warm color. *The Vision* lay practically unknown till parts of it were republished by Southey. Since then it has lapsed into a still deeper obscurity.[1]

In 1720, Croxall published anonymously *The Fair Circassian,* a poetic paraphrase of Solomon's Song. The Preface was dated " Oxon. 25 March 1720," and was avowedly written by a tutor who said that the real author had lately died — a form of literary deception by no means uncommon in the

---

[1] It is barely possible that Croxall took the hint for his Vision from Robert Greene's *Vision — Grosart's Edition of Greene,* Vol. XII. Greene sees Chaucer and Gower.

eighteenth century. This poem was exceedingly popular. It went through many editions, but it raised up a host of enemies for Croxall, on account of its voluptuousness. It is not the only one of Croxall's poems characterized by untheological carnality. It is written in the heroic couplet with a sprinkling of Alexandrines. In warmth of passion it is very unlike the stock phrases of contemporary poetry.

Some of the editions of *The Fair Circassian* had shorter poems appended. These are also in Croxall's glowing style. One of these — written in a Spenserian verse-form — has a not unpleasant musical flow. It is called *Florinda Seen While She Was Bathing.*[1] Two stanzas will suffice : —

> "Florinda, with her sister nymphs, undrest,
>   Within the channel of the cooly tide,
> By bathing sought to soothe her virgin breast,
>   Nor could the night her dazzling beauties hide :
> Her features, glowing with eternal bloom,
> Darted, like Hesper, thro' the dusky gloom.

> "Her hair bound backward in a spiral wreath
>   Her upper beauties to my sight betray'd ;
> The happy stream concealing those beneath,
>   Around her waste with circling waters play'd ;
> Who, while the fair one on his bosom sported,
> Her dainty limbs with liquid kisses courted."[2]

Mr. Gosse says that Croxall described his aim in poetry as being "to set off the dry and insipid stuff" of the age by publishing "a whole piece of rich glowing scarlet."[3] This is interesting, as it shows that his dislike of Augustan poetry was conscious and pronounced. He was, however, not more than half emancipated ; with all his fire and passion, his work

[1] There is nothing especially Romantic about the title — the Classicists were always seeing women bathing.

[2] Cibber, *Lives of the Poets*, Vol. V., page 288.

[3] *Eighteenth Century Literature*, page 139. I do not know in what connection Croxall made this remark ; his writings are not easy to find.

has many conventionalities. He has more significance as a
Spenserian.

We next come to the sturdy figure of Allan Ramsay (1686–
1758). Ramsay is perhaps best known as the editor of
miscellanies; but we are here concerned with his own poetic
productions. These are in some cases characterized by a
decided antipathy to the prevailing Classicism. He managed
to put some real life into the most artificial of all compositions
— the Pastoral. His *Gentle Shepherd* appeared in 172;.
What Ramsay thought of the conventional Pastoral may be
seen by the Preface to his miscellany, *The Evergreen*, 1724.
He said, in the old bards, "the morning rises as she does in
the *Scottish* horizon. We are not carried to *Greece* or *Italy* for
a Shade, a Stream or a Breeze. . . . I find not Fault with
those Things, as they are in *Greece* or *Italy:* But with a
*Northern Poet* for fetching his Materials from these Places, in
a Poem, of which his own Country is the Scene; as our
*Hymners* to the *Spring* and *Makers of Pastorals* frequently do."
There is a freshness and healthy natural life about the *Gentle
Shepherd*, which made it seem almost startlingly new to the
Augustans, accustomed as they were to the Theocritus-Vergil
pattern. The songs Ramsay introduced were fresh and sweet;
and many images taken directly from nature show where the
author's real inspiration lay. But unfortunately Ramsay — in
spite of his aggressive naturalness — was too much under the
influence of Pope and the rest to leave his pastoral drama
unblemished. He doubtless thought that in making the two
shepherd lovers turn out to be of noble blood, he would please
the public taste; to a modern reader this *dénoûment* is a
glaring fault. Again, after some most natural and beautiful
touches, he introduces didactic observations in the regular
Augustan manner. The freshness of this pastoral is thus
mingled with artificiality, another illustration of the power of
literary fashion even over those men who are most opposed
to it.

Ramsay had published a quarto of his poems in 1721, and in 1731 appeared the first collected edition of his works. The Preface to this edition contains some matter not uninteresting. He says, " I shall never quarrel with any man whose temper is the reverse of mine, and enters not into the taste of the same pleasures. . . . Every man is born with a particular bent, which will discover itself in spite of all opposition. Mine is obvious, which since I knew, I never inclined to curb; but rather encouraged myself in the pursuit, though many difficulties lay in my way." He apologizes for his Scotch songs. " Such pedants as confine learning to the critical understanding of the dead languages, do not view me with a friendly eye. . . . That I have exprest my thought in my native dialect, was not only inclination, but the desire of my best and wisest friends; and most reasonable, since good imagery, just similes, and all manner of ingenious thoughts, in a well laid design, disposed into numbers, is poetry." This is an interesting definition.

Again he says, "Throughout the whole I have only copied from nature, and with all precaution have studied . . . not to repeat what has been already said by others." All this gives us evidence of Ramsay's originality, and defiant spirit; but his inability to free himself entirely from contemporary thought is shown by the fact that along with his nature-poetry he published imitations of Horace, and in another part of the Preface, he says, "Anacreon, Horace and Waller were poets, and had souls warmed with true poetick flame." Such mention of Waller is damnatory evidence against any complete break with Classicism on Ramsay's part. Some of Ramsay's songs, however, as *The Last Time I Came o'er the Moor, The Lass of Patie's Mill, Bessie Bell*, and *The Young Laird* are significant as forerunners of the songs of Burns, and we know that Burns had a high regard for Ramsay's work.[1] Principal Shairp speaks highly of Ramsay's services to the poetry of nature;[2] and

---

[1] " Yes! there is ane! a Scottish callan —
     There's ane; come forrit, honest Allan!"

[2] *Poetic Interpretation of Nature*, pages 194–196.

Veitch says, " Allan Ramsay is by far the most interesting and influential literary personage in Scotland in the first half of the eighteenth century. . . . Ramsay had the courage, in a conventional time both in English and Scottish poetry, to recognize and be true to the manners, the simple every-day life, the rural character, and the scenery of his native land." [1] Had Ramsay never come into so close personal contact with the Augustans, he might have done much bolder and more original work than he did.[2]

The last author we shall treat in the contemporary reaction is William Hamilton of Bangour (1704–1754). Hamilton was like Parnell in his quiet, retiring disposition. The first collection of his poems was not published till 1748, and then during the author's absence from the country. It was published anonymously, with a preface by Adam Smith, the economist. A reprint of this edition appeared in 1749. In 1758 a new edition was published bearing the author's name. In 1760 came the only edition marked by any accuracy or completeness; and his fame was immediately assailed by the *Monthly Review* (February, 1761), which sneered at his poetical ability. After that there was no new edition of Hamilton — although he was reprinted once or twice — until 1850. Hamilton has thus never enjoyed a wide reputation; but during his life-time he was well known within a small circle, and regarded with high admiration. He was something of an aristocrat and in his temperament not unlike the poet Gray. He was a lonely scholar, fond of solitude and books, and disliked publicity as sincerely as his great contemporary. Among much incomparably wretched trash, he wrote some excellent pieces, and one thoroughly Romantic ballad, *The Braes o' Yarrow.* Allan Ramsay, although barred from Hamilton's

---

[1] *The Feeling for Nature in Scottish Poetry*, Vol. II., page 24.

[2] Ramsay was on intimate terms with the great Classicists; the last poem in Vol. I. of the *Tea-Table Miscellany* (1724) is called *The Quadruple Alliance*, and he says:

> "Swift, Sandy, Young and Gay,
> Are still my heart's delight,"

circle by social inferiority, exerted a strong influence upon him; and his influence was all for good. It was Ramsay who first brought *The Braes o' Yarrow* into public attention, by publishing it in his *Tea-Table Miscellany*. This poem is not only lyrically melodious, but is full of the spirit and fire of the old ballads. It is by all odds the best thing Hamilton ever wrote, as well as the most Romantic in tone.

Like Parnell, Hamilton handled the octosyllabic couplet with great ease, and did some excellent work in this measure. Some of his nature-poetry will bear quoting. In his poem, *Contemplation* (probably written in 1739) he shows something of the Wordsworthian spirit : —

> " Above, below, and all around,
>     Now naught but awful quiet's found,
>     The feeling air forgets to move,
>     No zephyr stirs the leafy grove,
>     The gentlest murmur of the rill
>     Struck by the potent charm is still,
>     Each passion in this troubled breast
>     So toiling once lies hush'd to rest,
>     Whate'er man's bustling race employs,
>     His cares, his hopes, his fears, his joys,
>     Ambition, pleasure, interest, fame,
>     Each nothing of important name,
>     Ye tyrants of this restless ball,
>     This grove annihilates you all.[1]
>     Oh power unseen, yet felt, appear !
>     Sure something more than nature's here.
>     Now on the flow'ring turf I lie,
>     My soul conversing with the sky."

After this singularly fine passage, which, in its day, was a real contribution to nature-poetry, he wanders off into dreamy moralizing, after the fashion of Pope.

---

[1] *Cf.* Marvell, in *The Garden:*

> "Annihilating all that's made
>     To a green thought in a green shade."

Hamilton seems to have had a great deal of force and passion which he deliberately repressed — perhaps thinking the age would not stand it — perhaps himself ashamed of it. This fact is curiously well shown by the 1850 edition of his poems.[1] His ode to Fancy is there published, and along with it a MS. copy which the author had written, but for some reason had withheld from the public. The MS. copy differs considerably from the printed one, especially in its franker expression of passion. Here is a passage from the suppressed draft, which appeared in print entirely changed and subdued : —

> " And now I gaze o'er all her charms,
>   Now sink transported in her arms ;
>   Fierce to her lips my lips I join,
>   Fierce in amorous folds we twine ;
>   Fierce in rage of love compressed,
>   Swells throbbing to the touch her breast.
>   Thus rioting in bliss supreme,
>   Might I enjoy the golden dream !
>   But ah ! the rapture will not stay,
>   For see, she glides, she glides away ! "

Hamilton was an ardent admirer of Milton, and some of his verses will be considered again among the poets of the Miltonic group. He was a good ballad-maker, writing in a vein strikingly Romantic, he had genuine passionate force which he hardly dared to express, he " unlocked his heart " in his nature-poetry, and yet he wrote long stretches of perfectly smooth and perfectly flat heroic couplets.[2] With this poet, we close for the present the consideration of reactionary tendencies during the Augustan age. Gay might perhaps have been included, but in all probability whatever opposition he had to the Classicists was not at all serious.

---

[1] Page 55.

[2] For example, he started a long poem in twelve books, called *The Maid of Gallowshiels*. He never progressed further than into the second book. He wrote this in 1726, when he was possibly re-acting from Ramsay's influence. The poem is inexpressibly tedious.

# CHAPTER III.

## THE REACTION IN FORM.

ROMANTICISM may be considered in two distinct aspects — Subject-matter and Form. In the study of the English movement, the first is far more important; but the latter cannot be overlooked. Since Romanticism, like almost all literary fashions, started as a reaction, the forms in which the new school clothed their productions naturally differed from that which had been most common; and in this aspect especially the movement was wholly in the direction of freedom. Here we may agree with Victor Hugo, that Romanticism is nothing but liberalism in literature. The same spirit that in other times and places rebelled against the Unities in dramatic art, struggled successfully in England with the tyranny of the Heroic Couplet in poetry. By 1726 the sovereignty of the Couplet was doomed, though for the rest of the century it lived and spasmodically flourished. It did not seem to occur to the Romanticists to make their reforms within the limits of the Couplet; that is, to return to the loose, overflowing couplets of the early seventeenth century. This would have brought the rebels even more squarely at issue with the reigning dynasty, and would have precipitated a conflict which the early reformers did not seek, and which they would have shrunk from entering upon. English poetry had to wait for Keats, to see the Heroic Couplet used in the field of Romanticism, and manipulated in direct defiance of the practice of Waller, Dryden and Pope.

The early Romanticists do not seem to have shown much direct opposition to the Couplet — they were simply weary of its monotony, and instinctively turned to other and freer forms of versification. Blank Verse, Octosyllabics, and the Spenserian stanza were the principal vehicles of expression which the new school adopted. These were in a way also associated with the Subject-matter aspect of Romanticism, for the first two of these forms owed much of their popularity to the powerful influence of Milton, and the third to the growing study and appreciation of Spenser. Indeed, Blank Verse came to be distinctly associated with the Romantic movement — its freedom giving a wider scope to the imagination than the closed couplets of the Classicists. Dr. Johnson and his ally Goldsmith perceived this fact, and accordingly threw the whole weight of their influence against blank verse ; while the liberals defended it, notably the poet Young, who grew more intensely radical as he advanced in years.

John Philips's *Cyder* appeared in 1706 ; his *Splendid Shilling* in 1705 ; it had been surreptitiously printed even earlier. Philips, of course, had been influenced by Milton and wrote in a pseudo-Miltonic style. On the title-page of the *Splendid Shilling* were the words *An Imitation of Milton*, and *Cyder* begins : —

> " What soil the apple loves, what care is due
> To orchats, timeliest when to press the fruits,
> Thy gift, Pomona, in Miltonian verse
> Adventurous I presume to sing."

Philips deserves mention here because he took to blank verse so early, and because twenty-five years later his example was much more influential than the intrinsic merit of his work justified. After Philips, the next important poem in blank verse was Thomson's *Winter*, which appeared in 1726, followed by *Summer* in 1727, and *Spring* in 1728. *Autumn* was first published with *The Seasons* in 1730. Thomson does not seem to have talked very much about his reasons for choosing blank verse ; he probably did not do so out of particular conscious hostility to the Couplet, though he was doubtless weary of its monotony. Possibly one of his reasons for forsaking the

Couplet was the fact that Pope had brought it to its utmost
refinement and polish, and that it was not capable of any
further development.    There is an interesting passage in
*Autumn* which shows that Thomson had a distinct preference
for blank verse, and also evidences the influence of Philips's
example : —

> "Philips, facetious bard, the second thou
>     Who nobly durst, in rhyme-unfettered verse,
>     With British freedom sing the British song."

Although the influence of Philips was out of all proportion
to his worth, his fame was not great enough to give sufficient
prestige to the verse-form he adopted ; but when Thomson
used it for *The Seasons*, the case was different.    Others felt
free to follow in his wake.    Somerville's *Chase* appeared in
1735, and Mr. Gosse says that "he delayed writing it so long
that we find his old Addisonian style tempered by the new and
freer manner of Thomson." [1]

Dyer's *Ruins of Rome* appeared in 1740.    Dyer thought the
*Ruins of Rome* bore about the same relation to *Grongar Hill*
as *Paradise Lost* to *L'Allegro*.    The poem begins : —

> "Enough of Grongar and the shady dales
>     Of winding Towy, Merlin's fabled haunt,
>     I sung inglorious.   Now the love of arts,
>     And what in metal or in stone remains
>     Of proud Antiquity," etc.

But posterity — so far as it has expressed any opinion — has
preferred *Grongar*.

The first installment of Young's *Night Thoughts* was given
to the world in 1742 ; by 1745 it was all published.    Young
was an older man than Thomson, but his chief poem came over
a decade later than *The Seasons*.    The style shows traces of
both Milton and Thomson ; of the former in the swelling

---

[1] *Eighteenth Century Literature*, page 138.   Mr. Gosse gives the date of this poem
as 1734.

magnificence of some of the lines, and of the latter in its somewhat even regularity. It should be said that both Thomson
and Young show the influence of the Classic measure ; many
of the lines are simply unrimed couplets. They could not
completely shake off the shackles in their versification, any
more than they could make a complete departure from Augustan
thought.

In 1743 appeared Robert Blair's *Grave*, a poem that he had
begun to work upon a number of years before. It is an interesting fact that this talented author should have written only [1]
one poem, and written that in blank verse ; still more interesting
when we observe that his versification is not of the Miltonic-
Thomson order, but points back to the Elizabethan age.[2]
Blair's verse is very loose and free, and bears evidence on every
page of the reading of old dramatists ; in the great number of
feminine endings, I think I detect particularly the influence of
Fletcher. *The Grave* was originally written before 1731, and
may have been begun independently of Thomson's example.
If so, it is another instance of the symptoms of revolt. Blair
was naturally more free from the reigning literary fashion for
two reasons ; he was a Scotchman, and he was young. The
young Scotchmen of those days were fond of reading in old
English authors and in the open book of Nature — two sources
of inspiration less familiar to their southern neighbors.

In 1744, Dr. Mark Akenside published his *Pleasures of Imagination*. This was a didactic poem in three books, which the
author afterward laboriously rewrote without improving. The
blank verse is both cold and heavy, though occasionally relieved
by fine passages. The poem is really Romantic only in its title.
One thing is noticeable about Akenside's poetry ; he was fond
of experimenting in various forms of versification, but he never
used the Heroic Couplet except once, and then in his *Re-
monstrance of Shakespeare* (1749), which, being put in the shape
of a theatre prologue, naturally took the couplet form.

---

[1] With the exception of an unimportant elegy.
[2] Mr. Saintsbury notices this in Ward's *English Poets*, Vol. III., page 217.

In the same year with the *Pleasures of Imagination* (1744),
appeared *The Art of Preserving Health*, by John Armstrong
(1709–1779). This is a blank-verse poem in four books.
Armstrong is a direct imitator of Thomson, and like Akenside,
was a physician. It should also be noted that he was a
Scotchman, and showed his love for old English authors by
some juvenile imitations of Shakspere. The longest of these,
a poem on Winter, was written while the young man was
passing the winter in a wild, solitary part of the country, and
curiously enough, seems to have been finished just as Thomson's poem on the same subject appeared. Whether either
borrowed from the other or not is uncertain ; but when Thomson by some means managed to read Armstrong's piece, he
showed it to David Mallet and others ; Mallet immediately
asked Armstrong's permission to print it ; the latter, not unwill-
ingly, consented. Then Mallet calmly suppressed it and it
was not published till 1770. The poem shows considerable
promise.

Besides these imitations of Shakspere, Armstrong, as is well
known, contributed a few Spenserian stanzas to *The Castle of
Indolence.*

In 1757 appeared *The Fleece*, by John Dyer (died 1758).[1]
This is a blank-verse poem in four books. Dyer was a
Welshman with a genuine love for natural scenery, which
came out plainly in his early octosyllabics, *Grongar Hill* and
*The Country Walk* (1726). He did not handle blank verse
with anything like the skill he showed in the shorter rimed
measure ; perhaps this was partly owing to the unpoetical
nature of the subjects he undertook.

A pronounced imitator of Thomson's blank verse was his
friend and fellow-countryman David Mallet (1700-02—1765).
He is chiefly famous for his connection with the ballad of

[1] The year of Dyer's birth seems not to be known: Dr. Johnson says he was born
in 1700. Dowden says 1698 or 1699. Leslie Stephen says "1700 or a year or two
previously." Ryland gives 1700 with a question-mark.

*William and Margaret*, which he seems still to have the credit of writing, though it can be clearly shown that he stole it.[1] Mallet published two lengthy poems in blank verse, *The Excursion* (1728) and *Amyntor and Theodora* (1747). *The Excursion* particularly shows Thomson's influence; its verse has many similarities to that of *The Seasons*, and it has much to say about nature, although its author is evidently insincere. The style is extremely "classic" in its cold, argumentative, viscous flow. Both poems are wofully tedious. Joseph Warton said of *Amyntor and Theodora*, "The nauseous affectation of expressing everything pompously and poetically, is nowhere more visible than in a poem lately published, entitled *Amyntor and Theodora*."[2]

The next blank-verse poem of considerable reputation that followed Dyer's *Fleece*, was *The Sugar Cane* (1764), by Dr. James Grainger, (1721 (?)–1766). This was of course in the didactic style. Grainger was an intimate friend of Percy, and their correspondence on the *Reliques* and on *Ossian* is of much more value and importance for our purposes than Grainger's blank verse.

The poems above mentioned are the chief essays in blank verse that appeared in England between 1700 and 1765. There were, of course, shorter poems of importance, such as Joseph Warton's *Enthusiast*, written in 1740. The Heroic Couplet was not abandoned during this period, but the more knowing ones let it alone, and many of the lesser lights took to blank verse because it was the fashion. Mr. Perry says, "Doubtless blank verse was a reaction against the couplet. It was the first sign of a protest against that rigid form, just as in Milton's hands it was the last measure in which a poet of heroic proportions spoke to the world. Yet the instrument he commanded the puny bardlings of the last century could not handle; his dignity was mimicked by a feeble rumble. . . . Yet they felt the charm of his verse; that was something, and

---

[1] See Appendix.      [2] Essay on Pope, Vol. I., page 147.

they maintained their side with obstinacy in the face of violent opposition." [1]

The Octosyllabic Couplet had not been entirely neglected in the Augustan age, although, of course, it was nothing like so common as the prevailing decasyllabic measure.  I have spoken of Parnell's skillful manipulation of it; [2]  Dyer used it gracefully and won a wide reputation, which he still holds among students.  William Hamilton of Bangour did excellent work with the measure ;  and the whole Miltonic school, their heads full of *L'Allegro* and *Il Penseroso*, scribbled octosyllabics all through the middle of the century.

We have seen that the reaction in form most naturally took the shape of blank verse for long poems ;  so that the sympathizers with the Romantic movement, consciously or unconsciously, found themselves defending blank verse, while the Classicists attacked it vigorously.  Dr. Johnson's opinions on the subject are well known ;  it is, however, worth noticing here that in the year 1759 two of the most celebrated poets of the century came out positively on opposite sides — Goldsmith and Young.  There was, so far as I know, no intentional opposition between them, but it is an interesting fact that opinions so exactly contrary should have appeared at the same time, and from the pens of so eminent men.  Goldsmith's *Inquiry into the Present State of Polite Learning* was published in April, 1759.  In its pessimistic note, and contempt for the revival of old English authors, it is in even more striking contrast with Young's buoyant essay.  Chapter XI. of Goldsmith's wail is particularly interesting — *On the Marks of Literary Decay in France and England*.  The present state of literature with the fondness for blank verse, he emphatically condemns.  "From this proceeds the affected security of our odes, the tuneless flow of our blank verse, the pompous epithet," etc. [3]

1 *Eighteenth Century Literature*, page 384.

2 See page 27.

3 Goldsmith was, of course, largely influenced by Dr. Johnson.

Young's *Conjectures on Original Composition* took the form of an open letter to the "author of Sir Charles Grandison." Young was 77 years old when he wrote this essay, which makes all the more remarkable its breadth of thought and sprightliness of treatment.[1]  Young's main purpose in writing the essay was to stir up the age to original composition, and its buoyant optimism is in striking contrast to Goldsmith's dismal utterances; but in the course of his remarks Young also took occasion to discuss the relative merits of blank verse and rime.  He pronounces his opinion in the most emphatic style.  Speaking of Pope's translation of Homer, he says. "Had Milton never wrote, Pope would have been less to blame; but when in Milton's genius, Homer, as it were, personally rose to forbid Britons doing him that ignoble wrong, it is less pardonable, by that effeminate decoration, to put Achilles in petticoats a second time.  How much nobler had it been, if his numbers had rolled on in full flow, thro' the various modulations of masculine melody, into those grandeurs of solemn sound which are indispensably demanded by the native dignity of heroic song !  How much nobler if he had resisted the temptations of that Gothic demon [2] which modern poesy, tasting, became mortal ! . . .  Harmony, as well as eloquence, is essential to poesy; and a murder of his music is putting half Homer to death.  'Blank' is a term of diminution ;  what we mean by 'blank verse' is verse, unfallen, uncursed ;  verse reclaimed, re-inthroned in the true language of the gods ;  who never thundered, nor suffered their Homer to thunder, in rhyme." [3]  Again, speaking of Dryden, he says, "The strongest demonstration of his no-taste for the buskin are (*sic*) his tragedies fringed with rhyme ; which, in epic poetry is a sore disease, in the tragic absolute death.  To

---

[1] It is rather singular that this significant piece of eighteenth century prose should be at present so neglected.  It is in Vol. II., of Young's Complete Works, London, 1854.  The page references that follow are to this edition.

[2] Rime.

[3] *Conjectures*, page 565.

Dryden's enormity, Pope's was a slight offence. . . . 'Must rhyme,' then say you, 'be banished?' I wish the nature of our language could bear its entire expulsion; but our lesser poetry stands in need of a toleration for it; it raises that, but sinks the great; as spangles adorn children, but expose men." [1]

Young's preference for blank verse was certainly distinctly marked, and the essay is especially suggestive coming at this time, as it shows how the Romantic movement was having its effect on the poet's mind. He would not have written like that in the first quarter of the century, when he was polishing off couplets along with the Augustans.

No discussion of the Reaction in Form would be complete without noticing the disappearance of the Sonnet, and its subsequent revival. The sonnet is as naturally a form for Romantic poetry, as the couplet was for Classic. Imagine the *Essay on Man* put into a sonnet sequence, like Rossetti's *House of Life!* Whatever the sonnet may be best fitted for, it is certainly wholly unfit for wit, satire, and didactic verse. It is, therefore, not at all surprising that the sonnet should have been almost completely neglected by the Augustans. It is fair to say that it practically disappeared. The only sonnet written in English between the performances of Milton, and Gray's sporadic attempt in 1742, that has survived, is a sonnet on Death, written, curiously enough, by Pope's mentor, William Walsh. The form of this sonnet is extremely irregular; [2] it has, however, some excellent lines, though the sentiment is Augustan. With the exception of this lonely sonnet, none of the Classicists, so far as we know, tried their hand at this form of verse. They would undoubtedly have ridiculed it. In 1742, Gray wrote a fine sonnet on the death of his brilliant

[1] *Conjectures*, page 574.

[2] The riming scheme is *ab, ab, bc, bc, dd, ce, ec.* This sonnet was written before 1708, for Walsh died in that year. Mr. Gosse erroneously says (Ward's *English Poets*, III., 7) that it is the only sonnet written in English between Milton's and Warton's!

friend, Richard West, but it was not published till after Gray's death. This is also irregular in form,[1] and has a few classicisms, which brought down a most unwarrantably severe judgment from Wordsworth.

About the middle of the century the sonnet was revived by Thomas Edwards, Benjamin Stillingfleet, Thomas Warton, and William Mason. No one of these men can claim the sole credit of its revival;[2] but Edwards deserves praise for his persistence in sonnet composition, and Warton by his greater influence helped to make the sonnet fashionable.

The sonnets of Benjamin Stillingfleet (1702-1771) were great neither in number nor in excellence, but some of them were certainly written before 1750, which gives their author a place among the pioneers. Mason said that he himself wrote a sonnet in 1748, and it is so dated in his works; but Mason was so loose in his statements that he cannot always be relied upon. However, he wrote a number of sonnets before 1750. Thomas Warton wrote nine sonnets, all on the Miltonic model.[3] Some of these were written about the year 1750.

One of the most interesting, although almost entirely neglected men among the sonnet revivers, was Thomas Edwards (1699-1757). Edwards was famous in his own day for a bitter controversy with Warburton, over the latter's edition of Shakspere. In 1747, when that work appeared, Edwards came out with a Supplement.[4] It was a merciless exposure of Warburton's editorial methods. Many of the literary men of the day became interested in the fight; Akenside warmly supported Edwards, and wrote a poem on

---

[1] Rimes *ab, ab, ab, ab, cd, cd, cd.*

[2] Mr. Ward says (*English Poets*, III., 383) that Warton revived the sonnet, but this statement taken by itself is not strictly true.

[3] The influence of Milton was doubtless one of the chief causes of the sonnet revival. His minor poetry was extremely popular about 1750.

[4] A Supplement to Mr. Warburton's Edition of Shakespear. Being the Canons of Criticism, and Glossary. By another Gentleman of Lincoln's Inn. London, 1748. After the 3d edition, the book was called *The Canons of Criticism.*

the subject.[1]   In the third edition of *The Canons of Criticism*
(1750), Edwards printed two sonnets by himself.   In the fifth
edition (1753) five sonnets appeared ;  and along with the
seventh edition (1765), besides the five sonnets previously
mentioned, Edwards's editor published forty-five other sonnets,
some of which Edwards had printed in Dodsley's *Miscellanies*.
Edwards was thus the author of just fifty sonnets.   These
are chiefly addressed to his private friends, and are not particularly remarkable for their literary merit.   What is remarkable is the fact that Edwards persistently wrote in this form
at a time when it was so unfashionable.   Forty-six of these
sonnets are on the Miltonic model, and the other four are
after the Spenserian pattern — a curious fact, as the Spenserian
sonnet has never been at all popular.   Edwards's masters were
Spenser and Milton ;  in one of his sonnets he calls Spenser
"the sweetest bard that ever sung" ;  and there are many
complimentary allusions to Spenser, Shakspere, and Milton.
All of Edwards's poetical works that I have been able to find,
consist of these fifty sonnets, and one epistolary ode.   The
sonnet was evidently his favorite mode of expression, and
the early date at which he wrote them ought to give him a
much more prominent place among the sonnet revivers than
he has thus far obtained.[2]

Not long after 1760, when Romanticism was a living force,
the sonnet became exceedingly popular ;  so that the century
closed with the sonnet as exalted as it had been despised among
the Augustans.   The disappearance and revival of this verse-
form were certainly outward indications of the reaction against
the couplet, and the general growth of the Romantic movement.

I have in this chapter sketched in a necessarily cursory
fashion, the Reaction in Form as expressed in blank verse,
octosyllabics, and the sonnet ;  the Spenserian revival is so
important as to deserve a much more thorough treatment
in a separate chapter.

[1] Akenside's *Odes*, Book II., Ode X.   This poem appeared in 1751, on Warburton's
Edition of Pope.

[2] I have since seen two sonnets of Edwards, one dated 1746, the other 1747.

# CHAPTER IV.

## THE SPENSERIAN REVIVAL.

FRENCH ROMANTICISM in its early stages was wonderfully fortunate in having the aid of an original genius — Victor Hugo. He had enough creative power in his own intellect and imagination to supply the Romantic movement with all the material it needed. But in the beginnings of English Romanticism there was no supreme, dominating figure. Instead of striking out into wholly new paths, the men who led the movement naturally looked back to the past to find the inspiration the lack of which was so plainly evident in the present. Among the old English poets, it was Spenser who supplied them with just what they sought. Spenser was the poet of Romanticism as Pope was of Classicism. They stand exactly in opposition; the latter all intellect, didactic and satirical; the poet of town life and of fashionable society; the former all imagination and exaggeration; the poet of dreamland, of woods and streams, of fairy and supernatural life. Along with the sharp contrast in substance, there is also the pronounced difference in style. Nothing could be more unlike the regular strokes of the couplet than the lazily flowing melody of the Spenserian stanza.

Spenser thus played a most important part in the new movement — a part much greater than that of Shakspere and Milton — although both these poets were extreme favorites with the Romanticists. Spenser had not been wholly neglected in the Augustan age, as will presently be shown; but he was known only to the scholars and antiquarians, and not to the mass of literary men. As soon as he was really brought before the public, writers and readers turned to his pages with avidity — eager for that solace and refreshment which the dry bones of Classicism could no longer afford.

But there is one exceedingly important fact to notice in the multitude of Spenserian imitations — *very few men took him seriously*. They read him for amusement, and they practised his versification for amusement; this fact explains why so many satires and so much half-comic poetry were written in the Spenserian form. The spirit of the Augustan age lingered long after the zenith of its glory had been passed and affected nearly if not quite all of the Spenser imitators. Thomson — whose *Castle of Indolence* was immeasurably above all the other attempts in this stanza — thought it necessary to include plenty of mild satire in his poem; and Shenstone, when he first wrote *The Schoolmistress*, never dreamed of taking Spenser seriously, and was especially anxious that the public should not take his jest for earnest. The bulk of the Spenserian imitations were used for satire, parodies and "occasional" poetry.

But though this fact should never be forgotten by the literary student, it should also be remembered that the real influence of Spenser during these years was strong and healthy. Many people read him and loved him, who did not dare to confess themselves before men; and many who began by taking Spenser as a joke, were led to the serious study and appreciation of his poetry. To these he was the golden gate to the realms of romance; the splendors of chivalry, the military glory of the days of "ladies dead and lovely knights" — all this was rescued from oblivious contempt and made once more real. Thus the influence of Spenser, which after inspiring Milton, had lain dormant through the Classical period, again asserted itself as a powerful quickening force. By the middle of the century, it was so much the fashion to write in the stanza and to use old English words, that many insignificant poetasters dipped into the *Fairy Queen* just deep enough to get the swing of the stanza and a small vocabulary of obsolete words.

Towards the end of the seventeenth century, two famous literary men expressed their opinions of Spenser in an interesting manner. Sir William Temple, in his Essay *Of Poetry*, said, "Spencer endeavoured to make Instruction instead of Story, the Subject of an *Epick* Poem. His Execution was excellent, and his Flights of Fancy very noble and high, but his Design was poor, and his Moral lay so bare, that it lost the Effect; 'tis true, the Pill was gilded, but so thin, that the Colour and the Taste were too easily discovered." [1]

Addison seems to have had this passage of Temple's in mind, when he wrote his lines on Spenser, in the famous *Account of the Greatest English Poets* (1694): —

> "Old Spenser next, warm'd with poetic rage,
> In ancient tales amus'd a barbarous age ;
> An age that yet uncultivate and rude,
> Where'er the poet's fancy led, pursued
> Through pathless fields, and unfrequented floods,
> To dens of dragons, and enchanted woods.
> But now the mystic tale, that pleas'd of yore,
> Can charm an understanding age no more ;
> The long-spun allegories fulsome grow,
> While the dull moral lies too plain below."

Compare the last line quoted with Temple's statement that Spenser's "moral lay so bare, that it lost the effect."

It is rather singular that the Spenserian imitations in the eighteenth century should have been started by an Augustan of the Augustans — the poet Matthew Prior (1664–1721). In 1706 appeared his *An Ode, Humbly Inscribed to the Queen, on the Glorious Success of Her Majesty's Arms. Written in Imitation of Spenser's Style.* His imitation was by no means a perfect one; it was in a ten-lined stanza, riming *ab*, *ab*, *cd*, *cd*, *ee*. It is, however, an extremely important poem, being the prototype of a great many of the Spenserian imitations that followed. Indeed, it is probable that some of the poetasters learned

---

[1] Miscellanea, Part II., *Of Poetry.*

all their Spenser through Prior. He seems to have been the originator of this pseudo-Spenserian stanza.[1] Curiously enough, his two masters in this Ode were the extreme leaders and models of the Classic and Romantic schools — Horace and Spenser. It sounds paradoxical to say that a poem can be written after the model of Horace and Spenser, but that is just what Prior attempted to do. In his interesting preface, he says, "As to the style, the choice I made of following the ode in Latin, determined me in English to the stanza; and herein it was impossible not to have a mind to follow our great countryman Spenser; which I have done (as well, at least, as I could) in the manner of my expression, and the turn of my number; having only added one verse to his stanza, which I thought made the number more harmonious; and avoided such of his words as I found too obsolete. I have, however, retained some few of them, to make the colouring look more like Spenser's." He then goes on to enumerate such words as "I weet," "I ween," *etc.* "My two great examples, Horace and Spenser, in many things resemble each other; both have a height of imagination, and a majesty of expression in describing the sublime; and both know to temper those talents, and sweeten the description, so as to make it lovely as well as pompous; both have equally that agreeable manner of mixing morality with their story, and that *curiosa felicitas* in the choice of their diction, which every writer aims at and so few have reached; both are particularly fine in their images, and knowing in their numbers."

I have quoted this preface somewhat at length, because it is so admirable an example of Queen Anne literary criticism; and exhibits just that confusion of ideals so often shown by the Augustans. His comparison of Horace and Spenser was accepted in gravity and good faith. His saying that by adding

---

[1] Donne and Phineas Fletcher had written ten-lined stanzas, ending with an Alexandrine, but not with this riming scheme. See Schipper's *Englische Metrik,* III., page 775.

a verse to Spenser's stanza he had made "the number more harmonious," sounds to us, and must have seemed to the Wartons, like unspeakable audacity; but Prior did not think so, and he displeased contemporary critics no more in this than when he put a fine old English ballad into the Heroic Couplet.

It is hardly necessary to add that Prior's ode is utterly destitute of Spenser's spirit. It is simply the familiar couplet with the riming scheme changed, and is if anything still more monotonous. It shows what the Augustan ideal of "harmony" in versification was. One stanza will suffice :—

> "When bright Eliza rul'd Britannia's state,
> Widely distributing her high commands,
> And boldly wise, and fortunately great,
> Freed the glad nations from tyrannic bands ;
> An equal genius was in Spenser found ;
> To the high theme he match'd his noble lays ;
> He travell'd England o'er on fairy ground,
> In mystic notes to sing his monarch's praise ;
> Reciting wondrous truths in pleasing dreams,
> He deck'd Eliza's head with Gloriana's beams."

Dr. Johnson's remarks on this imitation are well worth quoting : "His poem is necessarily tedious by the form of the stanza ; an uniform mass of ten lines thirty-five times repeated, inconsequential and slightly connected, must weary both the ear and the understanding. His imitation of Spenser, which consists principally in *I ween* and *I weet*, without exclusion of later modes of speech, makes his poem neither ancient nor modern." Johnson compared a stanza of Spenser's with one of Prior's to show "with how little resemblance he has formed his new stanza to that of his master. . . . By this new structure of his lines he has avoided difficulties ; nor am I sure that he has lost any of the power of pleasing ; but he no longer imitates Spenser." [1]

---

[1] *Life of Prior.*

Somewhere between 1713 and 1721 another Spenserian imitation appeared, which I am almost certain was written by Prior. The poem was called *Colin's Mistakes. In Imitation of Spenser's Style.* It is in the ten-lined stanza, with the same riming scheme as Prior's *Ode to the Queen* in 1706. Colin sees a maiden, whom he first supposes to be Pallas, then Juno, then Venus, but Clio finally informs him that it is Lady Henrietta Cavendish Holles-Harley. The thought is, of course, typically Augustan; but the allusions to Spenser are interesting. In the first stanza occur the words, —

> "And much he lov'd and much by heart he said
> What Father Spenser sung in British verse.
> Who reads that bard desires like him to write,
> Still fearful of success, still tempted with delight."

Other interesting references might be quoted. The exact date of this poem I have been unable to ascertain.[1]

Some interest in Spenser on the Pastoral side was aroused by Ambrose Philips (1671–1749), who was mainly inspired by Spenser in writing his *Pastorals* (1709). Dr. Johnson said in his *Life of Philips* that while Pope took Vergil for his pattern, Philips took Spenser.

Pope was not altogether lacking in appreciation of Spenser. In 1715 he wrote to Hughes, the editor of Spenser's works,

---

[1] Lady Henrietta Cavendish Holles married Edward Harley, the son of the Earl of Oxford, October 31, 1713. The poem must, therefore, have been written after that event, and at some time previous to 1721, the year of Prior's death. The poem is printed in Nichols's *Select Collection of Poems*, Vol. 7. Nichols adds a note, in which he states his belief that the poem was written not by Prior, but by Samuel Croxall. But it is extremely unlikely that Croxall should have written verses in praise of the daughter-in-law of the man whose administration he publicly satirized; and furthermore there are several strong reasons for Prior's authorship. Prior was a great friend of Edward Harley, spent many days at his house, and died there in 1721; in 1719 Prior wrote some *Verses* addressed to Lady Henrietta Cavendish Holles-Harley, the heroine of the poem here discussed; and lastly, *Colin's Mistakes* is in exactly the same measure as Prior's *Ode* in 1706, a measure which Croxall to my knowledge never handled. These reasons seem to me to be very strong evidence for Prior's authorship.

"Spenser has been ever a favorite poet to me; he is like a mistress, whose faults we see, but love her with them all."[1] But his exceedingly coarse burlesque of the old poet shows that if his appreciation was sincere, he did not dare to avow it publicly. When *The Alley* was written seems difficult to ascertain. We know from Spence's *Anecdotes* that Gay had some slight share in its composition.[2] The poem stands among Pope's imitations of Chaucer, Waller, Cowley, and others, and we are told that they were "done by the Author in his Youth." Joseph Warton said that some of these imitations were written at fourteen or fifteen years of age.[3] In composing *The Alley* Pope was, of course, not prompted by his love for Spenser; it was simply an exercise in versification. The piece contains six stanzas, and is written in the regular stanza of the *Fairy Queen.*

Public attention was called to Spenser by Steele, in the *Spectator* for November 19, 1712.[4] Steele begins by remarking on the recent Miltonic criticisms, and then adds: "It is an honourable and candid endeavour to set the works of our noble writers in the graceful light which they deserve. You will lose much of my kind inclination towards you if you do not attempt the encomium of Spenser also, or at least indulge my passion for that charming author so far as to print the loose hints I now give you on the subject." He proceeds then to describe the general plan of Spenser's poem, and says: "His style is very poetical; no puns, affectations of wit, forced antitheses, or any of that low tribe.[5] . . . His old words are all true English." He then quotes several stanzas. How far Steele was prompted to all this by real

---

[1] *Works*, Vol. X., page 120.

[2] "'The Alley' in imitation of Spenser, was written by Mr. Pope, with a line or two of Mr. Gay's in it." — *Anecdotes.* Page 167 of Underhill's *Selection.*

[3] *Essay on Pope*, Vol. II., page 29. London, 1782.

[4] No. 540.

[5] This sounds like a hit at contemporary poetry; but of course he really means the "Metaphysicals" of the seventeenth century.

love of Spenser, or by the necessity of writing his sheet, is
hard to say; his remarks at any rate do not seem to have
caused much discussion.

In 1713 appeared *An Original Canto of Spencer, design'd as
part of his Fairy Queen, but never printed, now made publick by
Nestor Ironside.* This was written by Rev. Dr. Samuel Croxall,
previously alluded to.[1]    The Preface contains a fictitious
account of the supposed unpublished piece of verse; the
poem is in truth a satire against the Earl of Oxford's (Harley's)
administration.    The next year (1714) Croxall brought out
*Another Original Canto,* under the same assumed name.[2]
Croxall afterwards acknowledged the authorship of these
cantos, for his *Vision* (1715) mentions them on the title-page.
It is interesting to notice that he employed the Spenserian
stanza for the purpose of political satire.    In 1714 Croxall
also published an Ode to George I. on his arrival in England,
"written in the stanza and measure of Spenser."

In 1715 appeared the first eighteenth century edition of
Spenser's works, edited by John Hughes (1677–1720).    He
prefixed an essay on allegorical poetry and also some *Remarks
on the Faerie Queene.*[3]    Hughes, of course, assumes the apologetic attitude.    "That which seems the most liable to exception in this work is the model of it, and the choice the author
has made of so romantick a story. . . .    The whole frame of
it (The Fairy Queen) would appear monstrous, if it were to
be examined by the rules of epick poetry, as they have been
drawn from the practice of Homer and Virgil; but as it is
plain the Author never designed it by those rules, I think it
ought rather to be considered as a poem of a particular kind,
describing, in a series of allegorical adventures or episodes,
the most noted virtues and vices.    To compare it, therefore,
with the models of antiquity, would be like drawing a parallel

[1] See Chapter II.

[2] Two copies of the 1713 Canto (2d and 3d ed.) are in the Yale Library.    They
are very rare.

[3] My quotations from this are from the reprint in Todd's edition of Spenser.

between the Roman and the Gothick architecture. . . . It ought to be considered, too, at the time when our author wrote, the remains of the old Gothick chivalry were not quite abolished; it was not many years before that the famous Earl of Surry, remarkable for his wit and poetry in the reign of King Henry VIII., took a romantick journey to Florence, the place of his mistress's birth, and published there a challenge against all nations in defence of her beauty." [1] All this apology for Spenser's Romanticism — and that is just what he calls it — is interesting and significant. Not less so are his remarks on Spenser's versification. "As to the stanza in which the *Faerie Queene* is written, though the author cannot be commended in the choice of it, yet it is much more harmonious in its kind than the heroick verse of that age. . . . The defect of it in long or narrative poems is apparent; the same measure, closed always by a full stop, in the same place, by which every stanza is made as it were a distinct paragraph, grows tiresome by continual repetition, and frequently breaks the sense, when it ought to be carried on without interruption. With this exception the reader will, however, find it harmonious, full of well-sounding epithets, and of such elegant turns on the thought and words, that Dryden himself owned he learned these graces of verse chiefly from our author, and does not scruple to say, that 'in this particular, only Virgil surpassed him among the Romans, and only Mr. Waller among the English.'" [2]

In these remarks, Hughes impresses me as feeling a great deal more than he dared to express; he understood the temper of the age, and knew what he was about when he used Dryden and Waller to advertise his poet. But the fact that he approvingly quoted Dryden's utterance shows once more how strange was the Classicist's notion of harmony. The ears that never

---

[1] Pages 20–23. This expedition of Surrey's is now known to be mythical; probably based on a novel by Nash, and given currency by one of Drayton's epistles.

[2] Page 40.

grew weary of the eternal couplet, objected to the Spenserian stanza because it was monotonous! It was many years before their notion lost its force. It took a whole century more to bring out Leigh Hunt's frank statement: "I do not hesitate to say that Pope and the French school of versification have known the least on the subject, of any poets perhaps that ever wrote. They have mistaken mere smoothness for harmony." [1]

Hughes's edition of Spenser did not accomplish much toward making the poet popular; it was 1750 — thirty-five years later — before an edition of Spenser again appeared in England. [2]

The next Spenserian imitation to be considered was written by William Whitehead (1715–1785), afterwards poet-laureate — one of the dullest of all the dull poets of the eighteenth century. He wrote the *Vision of Solomon* when at school, probably about the year 1730. It is a short poem, written in the ten-line stanza, on Prior's model. It is not at all remarkable for poetic merit. Whitehead also wrote two odes to his friend Charles Townsend, written in a six-lined stanza. [3] These were probably done at a comparatively early age.

With the exception of Whitehead's little school exercise — and the date of that is uncertain — I have not succeeded in finding any imitation of Spenser published between Croxall's performances in 1714 and the marriage odes on Prince Frederick in 1736. The first attempts in Spenserianism do not seem, therefore, to have awakened much attention, or to have called out many imitators; after 1736, however, when the people were a little more inclined toward Romanticism, a flood of Spenserian imitations appeared.

[1] Preface to the *Story of Rimini*, page 13.

[2] It may be worth mentioning in passing that in 1734 the learned Dr. Jortin published *Remarks on Spenser's Poems*. They are of no special significance, and are devoid of interest from the literary point of view.

[3] *To the Honourable Charles Townsend* and *To the Same — On the Death of a Relation.* The riming scheme is *ab, ab, cc,* the last an Alexandrine. This measure was sometimes used by the Spenserians.

William Thompson is a poet almost completely forgotten
to-day, but he was one of the best of the Spenserians. Little
is known of his life; the dates of his birth and death are
uncertain; but he was born in the early part of the century,
and died before 1767. He was a careful and enthusiastic
student of the old English poets. From early youth he
admired Spenser and imitated him in three poems. Although
Thompson was really filled with the Romantic spirit, it is
worthy of note that he was also extravagantly fond of Pope
— another instance of the unconsciousness of English Romanticism.

Besides Thompson's Spenserian imitations, he wrote a
number of graceful songs, and his *Ode Brumalis* shows him
to have been an intense lover of Shakspere. He might also
have been classed among the blank-verse school, for he
wrote a long poem in that measure, with the not particularly
attractive title of *Sickness*.

In May, 1736, Thompson produced his *Epithalamium on
the Royal Nuptials*. This is in the regular stanza of the
*Fairy Queen* and has something of the master's spirit in
its sweetness and melody. One stanza will suffice to show
the nature of the poem: —

> " Her Thamis (on his golden urn he lean'd)
> Saluted with this hymeneal song,
> And hail'd her safe. Full silent was the wind,
> The river glided gently soft along,
> Ne whisperèd the breeze the leaves among,
> Ne love-learn'd Philomel out-trill'd her lay ;
> A stilness on the waves attentive hung,
> A brighter gladness blest the face of day,
> All nature 'gan to smile, her smiles diffus'd the May."

In the same year (1736) Thompson also wrote *The Nativity*,
which he modestly called *A College Exercise*. This is also in
the regular Spenserian stanza, and has some beautiful passages.
Two stanzas are worth quoting : —

" Eftsoons he spy'd a grove, the Season's pride,
    All in the centre of a pleasant glade,
    Where nature flourish'd like a virgin-bride ;
    Mantled with green, with hyacinths inlay'd.
    And crystal-rills o'er beds of lilies stray'd ;
    The blue-ey'd violet and king-cup gay,
    And new-blown roses, smiling sweetly red,
    Outglow'd the blushing infancy of Day,
    While amorous west-winds kist their fragrant souls away.

\*        \*        \*        \*        \*

But hark, the jolly pipe, and rural lay !
    And see, the shepherd, clad in mantle blue,
    And shepherdess in russet kirtle gay,
    Come dancing on the shepherd-lord to view,
    And pay, in decent-wise, obeysance due.
    Sweet-smelling flow'rs the gentle votaries bring,
    Primroses, violets, wet with morning-dew,
    The sweetest incense of the early spring ;
    A humble, yet, I weet, a grateful offering."

Such verses as these have evidently nothing in common
with the Augustan spirit. They belong to Romanticism in
substance as well as in form. They display not only a
study of old English poetry, but a real, unaffected love of
nature.

In 1757 Thompson published a volume of poems. It
contained the two shorter pieces already discussed, and also
his *Hymn to May*. It is uncertain when this was written —
probably after 1750. His Preface to this *Hymn* is suggestive.
He says : "As Spenser is the most descriptive and florid of
all our English writers, I attempted to imitate his manner in
the following vernal poem. I have been very sparing of the
antiquated words, which are too frequent in most of the
imitations of this author ; however, I have introduced a few
here and there, which are explained at the bottom of each

page where they occur.[1]  Shakespeare is the poet of Nature, in adapting the affections and passions to his characters; and Spenser in describing her delightful scenes and rural beauties. His lines are most musically sweet; and his descriptions most delicately abundant, even to a wantonness of painting; but still it is the music and painting of Nature.  We find no ambitious ornaments, or epigrammatical turns, in his writings, but a beautiful simplicity; which pleases far above the glitter of pointed wit. . . .  A modern writer, has, I know, objected against running the verse into alternate and stanza; but Mr. Prior's authority is sufficient for me, who observes that it allows a greater variety, and still preserves the dignity of the verse. As I professed myself in this canto to take Spenser for my model, I chose the stanza; which I think adds both a sweetness and solemnity at the same time to subjects of this rural and flowery nature.  The most descriptive of our old poets have always used it. . . .  I followed Fletcher's measure in his "Purple Island." . . .  The Alexandrine line, I think, is peculiarly graceful at the end, and is an improvement on Shakespeare's Venus and Adonis. . . .  I hope I have no apology to make for describing the beauties, the pleasures, and the loves of the season in too tender or too florid a manner. The nature of the subject required a luxuriousness of versification, and a softness of sentiment."

This extremely interesting preface has several points worth attention.  It shows that Thompson was in spirit a thorough-going Romanticist, but that he was compelled to assume the defensive attitude, and even to fortify his position with the Classic name of Prior.  He is evidently speaking to an audience whose good-will he has yet to win; and the nature of his defense suggests that he had some particular critic in mind, especially as he once speaks of a "modern writer."

---

[1] Some of the eighteenth century glossaries are significant as showing the general ignorance of old English; they often explained words that are to-day perfectly familiar.

This modern writer I believe to be Dr. Johnson, who attacked
Spenserianism in the *Rambler* in May, 1751.[1]  Thompson
comes out for Romanticism in three ways : (1) As a lover of
old English poetry ; (2) as a believer in "luxuriousness" of
versification, which the couplet could not afford ; (3) as a
sincere lover of nature.  A quotation from the *Hymn to May*
will show all this clearly enough : —

> " Her hair (but rather threads of light it seems)
>   With the gay honors of the Spring entwin'd,
>   Copious, unbound, in nectar'd ringlets streams,
>   Floats glittering on the sun and scents the wind
>   Lovesick with odors ! — now to order roll'd,
>   It melts upon her bosom's dainty mold,
>   Or, curling round her waist, disparts its wavy gold.

> " Young circling roses, blushing, round them throw
>   The sweet abundance of their purple rays,
>   And lilies, dip'd in fragrance, freshly blow,
>   With blended beauties, in her angel-face ;
>   The humid radiance beaming from her eyes
>   The air and seas illumes, the earth and skies,
>   And open, when she smiles, the sweets of Paradise." [2]

Another stanza is an apostrophe to beauty : —

> " Where lives the man (if such a man there be)
>   In idle wilderness or desert drear,
>   To beauty's sacred power an enemy ?
>   Let foul fiends harrow him ;  I'll drop no tear.
>   I deem that carl, by Beauty's power unmov'd,
>   Hated of Heaven, of none but Hell approv'd ;
>   O may he never love !  O never be belov'd !" [3]

There is an additional fact to be noted about Thompson'
Spenserian imitations.  He wrote in the stanza of the *Fair*

---

[1] No. 121.   This would place the date of Thompson's poem after 1751.
[2] Stanzas X. and XI.
[3] Stanza LIV.

*Queen* not for idle amusement, or to exercise his poetic ingenuity, but because his mind was richly stored with the treasures of old English poetry. He was one of the few ardent admirers of Spenser. He was so unlike the majority of his contemporaries, that even Chalmers thinks it necessary to say that Thompson's style had unfortunately not been sufficiently "chastened into simplicity by the example and encouragement of the moderns."

In the year 1736 appeared another poem on the marriage of Prince Frederick; this was also by a university man, Richard Owen Cambridge (1717–1802). It was published among a number of Oxford congratulatory verses on the same subject, which calls our attention for a moment to the influences of the universities on the Spenserian movement. Many of the early imitations came from Cambridge and Oxford men, some of them hardly out of their teens, an evidence that the youngsters with literary ambitions were turning for inspiration to the wells of old English poetry. This little ode by Cambridge is in the ten-lined stanza; although imitative of Spenser, it is not avowedly so. It contains nothing worthy of special remark; it is no better and no worse than average occasional poetry.

Some years later, however, Cambridge published a much closer imitation of the ancient poet. This is his *Archimage* (1742–1750).[1] The title is, of course, borrowed from Spenser's famous magician. The poem is in the regular Spenserian stanza, and is mildly humorous and satirical; it describes how the author (Archimage), with four of his boat's crew, took a lady for a ride on the river. It is a rather pretty bit of trifling, and the allegory is well sustained; the large number of obsolete words is noticeable. Cambridge lived in the country and cultivated his quiet tastes for letters and landscape gardening; he had also a wide circle of literary friends. In 1751 he removed to Twickenham — and there issued his most pretentious effort in poetry, the *Scribleriad*, a

[1] I have not been able to discover precisely the year.

mock-heroic poem in six books, written in the couplet. It
received on its first appearance scarcely any recognition, and
has even less to-day. Although Cambridge lived after the
close of the century, he does not seem to have been especially
affected by the Romantic movement. In his Spenserian
imitations, he simply followed a literary fashion ; but it should
not be forgotten that the writings of more or less insignificant
authors show the course of a literary movement better than
the productions of great men. In the latter there is always
originality ; in the former we find copying of popular models.
This shows the necessity as well as the justification of raking
over so many of the dust-heaps of the past.

In the *Gentleman's Magazine* for April, 1737, appeared this
little note : —

NEWCASTLE-UPON-TYNE, April 23.

"I hope, Sir, you'll excuse the following poem (being the performance of one in his sixteenth year) and insert it in your next magazine,
which will oblige

Yours, etc.,

MARCUS."

Following the note was published the poem, called *The Virtuoso ; in Imitation of Spencer's Style and Stanza.* The author
was a poet who soon afterward became famous, Mark Akenside (1721–1770). *The Virtuoso* is in the regular Spenserian
stanza, and is full of attempts at old English. It is a mild
satire, resembling Spenser only in form. It was Akenside's
first and last essay in the regular stanza of the *Fairy Queen;*
but he seemed in later years to admire Spenser, and wrote
three odes in a ten-lined pseudo-Spenserian stanza.[1]

In 1739 appeared *On the Abuse of Travelling ; A Canto, In
Imitation of Spenser.*[2] This was by Gilbert West (1700–05—
1756). Very little is known of West's life. He was a learned

---

[1] Book I., Ode IX., *To Curio*, 1744. Book II., Ode XIII., *To the Author of
Memoirs of the House of Brandenburg*, 1751. Book II., Ode XI., *To the Country
Gentlemen of England*, 1758. All these have the rather curious riming scheme,
*ab, ab, cc, de, ed*, the last being an Alexandrine.

[2] This poem is in Dodsley's Collection (1765), Vol. II., page 98.

man, and published a number of translations of Pindar's odes. The poem before us is a gentle satire on the effects of travelling abroad, and the temptations encountered. It is in the allegorical style. Archimago attempts to entice the Red Cross Knight from the love of fairy-land by showing him all manner of voluptuous temptations. The poem has more Romantic atmosphere than West's later work. One stanza will suffice to show its quality (XXII.) : —

> " And now they do accord in wanton daunce
> To join their hands upon the flow'ry plain ;
> The whiles with amorous leer and eyes askaunce
> Each damsel fires with love her glowing swain ;
> 'Till all impatient of the tickling pain,
> In sudden laughter forth at once they break,
> And ending so their daunce, each tender twain
> To shady bow'rs forthwith themselves betake,
> Deep hid in myrtle groves, beside a silver lake."

The last stanza of the poem closes as follows : —

> " So to his former wiles he turns him soon,
> As in another place hereafter shall be shown."

But West never fulfilled this promise.

The most interesting thing about this imitation is the glossary. He explains words that are to-day perfectly clear, thus showing the limitations of the vocabulary in his time. Such words as sooth, guise, hardiment, Elfin, prowess, wend, hight, dight, paramours, behests, caitiffs, etc., West translates in footnotes. The prevailing ignorance of Spenser is also shown by his careful explanations of "Una" and "Paynim."

Gray was much pleased with this poem. He wrote from Florence to his friend, Richard West, July 16, 1740: "Mr. Walpole and I have frequently wondered you should never mention a certain imitation of Spenser, published last year by a namesake of yours, with which we are all enraptured and enmarvailed."

In 1751 appeared Gilbert West's second imitation — *Educa-tion. A Poem; in Two Cantos. Written in Imitation of the Style and Manner of Spenser's Fairy Queen*.[1] This is much duller than the *Abuse of Travelling*. It narrates the struggles of the Knight with Custom and the final victory of the former. Its main interest lies in West's attack on the artificial method of gardening (Stanzas XVII.–XXIV.).

Dr. Johnson, in his *Life of West*, took occasion once more to attack the Spenserian school. He himself failed altogether to appreciate the movement, but some of his criticisms are perfectly sound, judged by the standard of the poetry which the Spenserians produced. Dr. Johnson saw in this style of poetry only the versifying of the curious; he said the "effect was local and temporary"; they "presuppose an accidental or artificial state of mind"; they are "proofs of great industry, and great nicety of observation, but the highest praise, the praise of genius, they cannot claim." He also said they were "only pretty, the plaything of fashion, and the amusement of a day." Much of this is strictly true; but in these playthings the Doctor failed to perceive any significance.

In 1739 also appeared *A New Canto of Spenser's Fairy Queen*, in folio. Perhaps this was inspired by Croxall's work in 1713–14.[2]

A curious and interesting figure in the group was Samuel Boyse (1708–1749). Boyse's life is far more interesting than his poetry. He was born in Dublin, and married at the age of twenty. In 1731 he published in Edinburgh *Translations and Poems*. He had many brilliant opportunities for advancement, all of which he wasted by almost inexplicable recklessness. Debts at length drove him from Edinburgh. He often had to beg for the smallest coins, and wrote verses in bed to obtain money for clothes and food. Although a dissolute vagabond, it is interesting to notice that he published in 1739 a long

---

1 Only one Canto was really published.

2 I have not been able to find any copy of this Folio nor the name of its author.

poem in the couplet called *The Deity*. Here he was following in the wake of the *Essay on Man*. Moralizing, didactic poetry had then lost little of its strong hold on popular attention, and Boyse, as Mr. Perry says, wrote "with a keen eye on his market." Boyse also modernized some of Chaucer's tales. Although totally destitute of Spenser's spirit, he made imitations at various times. He paraphrased part of Psalm XLII, "In Imitation of the Style of Spenser." These verses sound more like the couplet than like the *Fairy Queen*, being in six-lined stanzas, riming *ab, ab, cc*. In 1736–7 he published *The Olive; an Heroic Ode. . . . In the Stanza of Spenser*. This was an "occasional" poem, on the King's return to Great Britain. In the Preface, Boyse says he modeled his work on Prior's ode in 1706, affording still another instance of the long-continued influence of Prior's short poem. *The Olive* is far better than Prior's ode; but it also illustrates the unsuitableness of this stanza for occasional poetry; and to show how much appreciation of Spenser Boyse had, it is only necessary to observe that he couples Spenser with "tuneful Waller," "deathless Addison," and Pope! He speaks of Prior in the highest terms, saying that he is "content to follow his steps at a distance." He also has one interesting passage, which shows some originality: "Satire is, I know, the prevailing taste of the age, and for that I am not ashamed to own I have neither genius nor disposition."

In 1740 he published an *Ode Sacred to the Birth of the Marquis of Tavistock*. This is in the same ten-lined stanza. It is artificial and lifeless.

About the same year appeared another poem from his pen, *The Vision of Patience*. This was "sacred to the memory of Mr. Alexander Cuming, a Young Gentleman unfortunately lost in the Northern Ocean on his return from China, 1740." This work has not much poetic merit, but is written in the allegorical style. The stanza describing the abode of the Goddess of Silence may be worth quoting : —

"Here no invading noise the Goddess finds,
  High as she sits o'er the surrounding deep ;
But pleas'd she listens to the hollow winds,
  Or the shrill mew, that lulls her evening-sleep ;
Deep in a cleft-worn rock we found her laid,
  Spangled the roof with many an artless gem ;
Slowly she rose and met us in the shade,
  As half disturb'd that such intrusion came ;
But at her sister's sight with look discreet,
  She better welcome gave, and pointed each a seat."

Although it is quite possible that Boyse had no first-hand
knowledge of Spenser at all, that was not the case with his
greater contemporary, William Shenstone (1714–1763). *The
School-Mistress* is one of the best of the Spenserian imitations
and is often ranked next to the *Castle of Indolence*, though it
hardly deserves so high a place. Shenstone published a first
incomplete form of this poem in 1737 ; it appeared in final
shape in 1742. Fortunately, we are able to know exactly
what attitude Shenstone held toward Spenser ; it throws considerable light on the whole school. A careful search of his
correspondence reveals the fact that his imitation was not
written in any serious spirit, and his earnest declaration that
he was "only in fun," is exceedingly interesting. But the
more he read Spenser the more he liked him ; and as people
persisted in admiring *The School-Mistress* for its own sake, he
finally consented to agree with them, and in later editions
omitted the commentary explaining that the whole thing was
done in jest. At first he speaks of his poem as a "burlesque"
— a "ludicrous imitation." Writing to his friend Mr. Graves,
January 19, 1742, he says : "The true burlesque of Spenser
(whose characteristic is simplicity) seems to consist in a *simple*
representation of such things as one laughs to *see* or to *observe*
one's self, rather than in any *monstrous* contrast between
the thought and words."[1] Again, writing to the same man,

---

[1] *Works*, Vol. III. (1769), page 61.

December 24, 1741, he says: "Some time ago I read Spenser's Fairy Queen; and when I had finished, thought it a proper time to make some additions and corrections in my trifling imitation of him, The School-Mistress.—His subject is certainly bad, and his action inexpressibly confused; but there are some particulars in him that charm one. Those which afford the greatest scope for a ludicrous imitation are, his simplicity and obsolete phrase; and yet these are what give one a very singular pleasure in the perusal." [1]

We see by this that when *The School-Mistress* was first written, Shenstone knew nothing apparently of Spenser; and that when he did actually read him, he was charmed in spite of himself. As he did not dare to consider Spenser seriously, he tries to point out certain characteristics to explain the charm he felt in the *Fairy Queen*, without seeing that the real source of the fascination lay in the beauty of the poetry. In his early years Shenstone was very much of an Augustan. The age speaks through him again in a letter to Mr. Graves, June, 1742. "I am glad you are reading Spenser; though his plan is detestable and his *invention* less wonderful than most people imagine, who do not much consider the obviousness of allegory; yet, I think, a person of your disposition must take great delight in his *simplicity*, his good-nature, etc. . . . When I bought him first, I read a page or two of the Fairy Queen, and cared not to proceed. After that, Pope's Alley made me consider him ludicrously; and in that light, I think, one may read him with pleasure. I am now . . . from trifling and laughing at him, really in love with him. I think even the metre pretty (though I shall never use it in earnest); and that the last Alexandrine has an extreme majesty." [2]

It is fortunate that we have a letter like this, so clearly exhibiting the attitude of one of the best-known men of his time toward one of the greatest names in English literature. The patronizing tone toward Spenser is extremely suggestive;

[1] *Works*, Vol. III., page 63.  [2] *Ibid.*, Vol. III., page 66.

and the fact that Shenstone's gate to this Romantic field was the coarse burlesque of Pope, is certainly noteworthy. When Pope exercised his ingenuity in this style of versification, he little dreamed that he was opening a new world even to the men of his age. Shenstone's remark that he thought "even the metre pretty" needs no comment. His letter, in all its stupidity, betrays a much deeper appreciation of Spenser than the writer dared to show.

One more letter of Shenstone's must be quoted ; it shows his anxiety that the people should not mistake his burlesque for a thing done in earnest. The letter is written to Mr. Graves, but bears no date : [1] "I have added a ludicrous index, purely to shew (fools) that I am in jest ; . . . You cannot conceive how large the number is of those that mistake burlesque for the very foolishness it exposes (which observation I made once at the Rehearsal, at Tom Thumb, at Chrononhotonthologos ; all which are pieces of elegant humour). I have some mind to pursue this caution further ; and advertise it, 'The School-Mistress, &c.' A very *childish* performance everybody knows (*novorum more*). But if a person seriously calls this, or rather, burlesque, a childish or low species of poetry, he says wrong. For the most regular and formal poetry may be called trifling, folly, and weakness, in comparison of what is written with a more *manly* spirit in ridicule of it." [2]

This letter affords proof positive of Shenstone's lack of seriousness in imitating Spenser. It is somewhat surprising, after approaching the old poet in this spirit, that Shenstone should have succeeded as well as he did. *The School-Mistress* will probably always be known as his best production, and we are not surprised to find Gray saying in 1751 or thereabouts : "'The School-Mistress' is excellent in its kind and masterly." [3]

The book-seller, Robert Dodsley (1703–1764), published in 1742 an imitation of Spenser called *Pain and Patience;* the

---

[1] Probably written in 1742.          [2] *Works*, Vol. III., page 69.
[3] *Gray's Works*, ed. Gosse, Vol. II., page 219.

piece is metrically rough, has no merit of any kind, and bears no evidence of being consciously imitative. About 1744 he published six uninspired six-lined stanzas *On the Death of Mr. Pope*. All the stanzas end with the same Alexandrine, —

"With sounds to soothe the ear, with sense to warm the heart,"

a sentiment unfortunately not descriptive of Dodsley's effort.

In July, 1743, appeared *Albion's Triumph; An Ode on the Success of His Majesty's Arms*. All I have been able to discover of this poem is an extract of five stanzas printed in the *Gentleman's Magazine*, for July, 1743. The metre is fashioned after that of Prior — ten-lined stanzas, with Prior's riming scheme. The extract is guilty of no poetical beauty.

The poet William Mason (1725–1797), who had little originality, but who imitated first Milton and then Gray in an almost servile fashion, does not belong to the regular Spenserian group, but in his *Musaeus* (written 1744, published 1747), he introduced a few stanzas in Spenser's style. *Musaeus* was a monody on the death of Pope, and written in imitation of Milton's *Lycidas*. Different poets in *Musaeus* bewail Pope's death; Chaucer speaks in an imitation of old English, and Spenser speaks two stanzas after the metre of the *Shepherd's Calendar* and three stanzas in the style of the *Fairy Queen*. There is nothing remarkable about these imitations; they simply give Mason a slight connection with the movement. He figures in another branch of Romanticism.

Thomas Blacklock (1721–1791) was blind from early youth. While a young boy, his parents read the poets aloud to him, mainly Spenser, Milton, Prior, Addison, Pope, and Ramsay. He began to compose rimes at the age of twelve, and circulated his writings in manuscript. Blacklock simply followed contemporary fashions in his compositions; and he was born late enough to come partially under the influence of the new school. The philosopher Hume was greatly interested in this blind man, and in a letter written October 15, 1754, he says: "I have asked him whether he retained any idea of light or colors. He assured me that there remained not the least trace of them. I found, however, that all the Poets, even the most descriptive ones, such as Milton and Thompson, were read by him with Pleasure. Thomson is one of his favorites." [1]

Blacklock wrote verses in many different kinds of metres, but the poem that chiefly concerns us here is his *Hymn to Divine Love; In Imitation of Spenser*.[2] This is a short production in seven-lined stanzas, riming *ab*, *ab*, *bc*, *c;* a rather unusual measure. The poem is absolutely common-place. In his verses called *Philantheus*, Blacklock also introduced the same stanzaic form. The only interesting thing about Blacklock's imitation of Spenser is the evidence which it gives of the strength of this literary fashion; for Blacklock had no originality; he simply followed popular forms.

Christopher Pitt (1699–1748) was chiefly celebrated in his day and generation for his translation of Vergil, which Joseph Warton in point of scholarship compared favorably with Dryden's. Pitt published a thin volume of *Poems and Translations* in 1727; in one of these bits of verse he alludes to Spenser, but his *Imitation* was probably not written till a number of years later. This is in the vein of Pope's *Alley*, and may have been directly inspired by it. Its title is *The Jordan*, and the nature of its contents may be guessed by the opening line, —

"A well-known vase of sov'reign use I sing."

The poem is in the regular Spenserian form, and contains a number of obsolete words. In mechanism it is not unskilful, but in spirit is merely a coarse burlesque.

Gloucester Ridley [3] (1702–1774) published in April, 1747, in Dodsley's *Museum*,[4] a piece called *Psyche; or the Great*

---

[1] Spence's *Anecdotes*, page 448.

[2] Probably published in 1746.

[3] An interesting account of Ridley appears in the *Gentleman's Magazine* for 1774, page 505.

[4] The *Museum* lasted from March 29, 1746, to September 12, 1747, and was issued fortnightly.

*Metamorphosis. A Poem, written in imitation of Spenser.* The history of this poem is not uninteresting. " The origin of this is as follows : his friend, Mr. Spence, having lent him the works of Spencer, which he had never read, on returning them, our author sent Mr. Spence, as a fragment, the fifteen first stanzas of *Psyche*, without farther plan or design, as an exercise to imitate that writer. Mr. Spence pressed him to finish it ; he did so, and completed the canto. This was his excuse for adopting obsolete words." [1] Afterwards, Dodsley urged him to continue the *Metamorphosis ;* Ridley rather shrank from this task, evidently finding composition in the Spenserian stanza desperately hard work. His plan for the whole poem is interesting, as showing how he tried to combine the moralizing-didactic spirit of the age with the Romantic style of poetry. "As the first part of the *Metamorphosis* in one canto, was a kind of Paradise Lost, this was to be a Paradise Regained. His plan (a very important one) was a view of the general notions of religion, with respect both to the *credenda* and *agenda*, which prevailed in the world, out of the Jewish church, before the incarnation, cast into four cantos, under the general title of *Melampus, or the Religious Groves.* . . . The first canto is Fear, which is contrasted by Superstition ; the second Trust, which is opposed by Enthusiasm ; the third Love, with the origin of Idolatry ; the last Joy. In the first canto . . . Psyche was left changed into a caterpillar ; in the next she is married to Elf, and her progeny are Elves and Fairies." Ridley made slow work with this titanic task, and the inspiration deserted him so often that he was more than once tempted to throw the whole thing aside. The complete poem *Melampus* did not appear until after his death. It was published in 1781.

It is interesting to notice what a jumble the whole plan was ; imitative of Spenser in its stanza and allegory, imitative of Milton in its general plan, and yet full of the didactic style

[1] *Gentleman's Magazine*, 1774, page 505.

of the Augustan age.   The canto called *Psyche*, the only portion published in his life-time, has little poetic merit. It is imitative of Spenser only externally — in stanza and language.   The account of Ridley's life in the *Gentleman's Magazine* ends with a ludicrously ambiguous compliment : " He exchanged this life, for a better, in November 1774, aged 72, leaving a widow and some daughters. *His works follow him.*"

Bishop Robert Lowth (1710–1787), the learned divine and famous lecturer on Hebrew poetry, made one slight attempt at Spenserian verse.   His *Choice of Hercules* first appeared in Spence's huge tome *Polymetis* (1747), in the tenth dialogue. Hercules chooses between two female figures, Pleasure and Virtue, hesitating through several stanzas, but, of course, eventually taking Virtue.   The allegorical scheme of the poem is interesting, but Lowth, although an excellent critic of poetry, had no creative gift.   The versification of this piece is modeled after the Prior pseudo-Spenserian form.

In the same year (1747) appeared an anonymous quarto, *A New Canto of Spencer's Fairy Queen.   Now first published.*   This was by John Upton; the title, of course, was not really intended to deceive the public.   The poem contains forty-two stanzas, ten-lined, after Prior's model.   At the beginning is a short quotation in Spenser's style.   Obsolete words abound, and allegorical abstractions are plentiful.   Many phrases are taken almost bodily from Shakspere.[1]   It may be worth while to quote one of Upton's stanzas, to show his style : —

> " Thus talking, on the Neighbour Beach they find
>     A Bark, all in her gaudy Trim displaid ;
>   The silken Sails sung in the whistling Wind,
>       Courting the Knight on Board, who nought afraid
>     Springs deftly on the Deck ; when Archimage

[1] For example:
>    " And ever and anon the sheeted Dead
>      Did squeak and gibber thro' the myrksome Air." — Stanza VII.

A wondrous Pin takes in his cunning Hand,
   That mov'd, as if instinct with Spirit sage,
    The bounding Bark, which made the adverse Land ;
  Where a bright bevy stood of Females fair,
  All ready to receive them, blith and debonnair." [1]

In addition to Lowth's, Ridley's and Upton's imitations, the
year 1747 saw still another from the pen of Robert Bedingfield
died 1768). It first appeared in Dodsley's *Museum* for May,
1747. *The Education of Achilles* is a poem of fourteen stanzas,
in the regular Spenserian form. It has more poetic merit than
the common run of contemporary imitations. The fondness
for abstractions — so common at this time — is very noticeable. Modesty, Temperance, Fidelity, Benevolence, Exercise,
Experience and Contemplation all take a hand in the " Education of Achilles."

In 1748 Joseph Warton published in a thin volume the
poetical remains of his father, the Rev. Thomas Warton, who
died in 1745. This volume contains among other pieces
*Philander, an Imitation of Spencer*. It was occasioned by the
death of Mr. William Levinz, November, 1706. At what
date it was written I have been unable to ascertain; but it is
interesting as showing how honestly the Warton brothers came
by their fondness for Spenser. The poem is prefaced by a
garbled quotation from the dedication to Spenser's *Astrophel*
as follows : —

  " To You alone I sing this mournful Verse —
    Made not to please the living, but the Dead —
  To You, whose soft'n'd hearts it may empierse
    With Dolours — (if you covet It to read —
  And if in You found pittie ever place,
  May You be mov'd to pittie such a case."

*Philander* is a short poem, in six-lined stanzas, completely
destitute of poetic merit. It is interesting simply as coming
from the father of the Wartons, and because of its early date.

---

[1] Of course a reminiscence of Milton's *L'Allegro*.

In 1748 appeared by far the best poem of the whole Spenserian school, *The Castle of Indolence*, by James Thomson, who
died two months after its publication. This poem is not
simply an *external* imitation of Spenser, as in the stanza, the
obsolete words, and the allegorical form of the story; much
of it is genuine poetry, and has something of the Romantic
feeling and atmosphere of Spenser, as well as touches of
his melodious music. Thomson had perhaps been partially
inspired by Shenstone's *School-mistress;* for the opening words
of his Advertisement remind one of Shenstone's notions. He
says, "This poem being written in the manner of Spenser, the
obsolete words, and a simplicity of diction in some of the lines,
which borders on the ludicrous, were necessary to make the
imitation more perfect." We can only wish that Thomson had
seen fit to give free expression to his love for Spenser, and
omitted from his poem all the burlesque element. But the
fact that Thomson thought ludicrous touches necessary is a
fact too suggestive to be forgotten.

How early Thomson began to admire Spenser is hard to say.
It is an interesting fact that the allusion to Spenser in *The
Seasons* did not appear in the first edition (1730), but was
inserted later. The allusion referred to is in *Summer* and
runs as follows : —

> " The gentle Spenser, fancy's pleasing son,
> Who, like a copious river, poured his song
> O'er all the mazes of enchanted ground."

Perhaps this was inserted after Thomson had begun to have
in mind *The Castle of Indolence*. We know that he had this
intention as early as 1733 or 1734, for he writes in 1748, "After
fourteen or fifteen years, *The Castle of Indolence* comes abroad
in a fortnight." [1] Whether he had it simply in mind during
those years, or was actually composing it, is impossible to say.[2]

---

[1] Letter to Paterson, *Thomson's Works* (1847), Vol. I., page ci.

[2] On the evidence of the words of Thomson quoted above, Mr. Gosse makes the
surprising statement (*Eighteenth Century Literature*, page 225) that Thomson had

The first canto of *The Castle of Indolence* is much better than the second, and the opening stanzas of the first are perhaps the best part of the poem. There is some of the same atmosphere that appears in Tennyson's *Lotus-Eaters.*

Stanza thirty has distinctly a Romantic tone : —

> "As when a shepherd of the Hebrid-Isles,
>     Placed far amid the melancholy main,
>   (Whether it be lone fancy him beguiles ;
>     Or that aërial beings sometimes deign
>   To stand, embodied to our senses plain)
>     Sees on the naked hill, or valley low,
>   The whilst in ocean Phœbus dips his wain,
>     A vast assembly moving to and fro ;
> Then all at once in air dissolves the wondrous show."

It is noticeable that in one place Thomson speaks of "my master Spenser." [1]

The delicate shading of humour gives a certain charm to the poem, and some passages have an interest other than poetical or Spenserian. But throughout the work one is conscious of an entirely different atmosphere from that in most of the other imitations; there are some genuine touches of Romanticism. Thomson has always had full credit — perhaps too much — for his aid to nature-poetry in the *Seasons;* but his greater contribution to Romanticism does not seem to have attracted so much general attention. Joseph Warton immediately recognized the value of the poem. He said, "There are some who think it (poetry) has suffered by deserting these fields of fancy, and by totally laying aside the descriptions of magic and enchantment. What an exquisite picture has Thomson given us in his delightful Castle of Indolence." He then quotes the stanza beginning, "As when a shepherd of the Hebrid-Isles." "I cannot at present recollect

---

actually written *The Castle of Indolence* by 1733. Mr. Gosse's statement is a wholly unwarrantable inference.

[1] Canto II., stanza 52.

any solitude so romantic, or peopled with beings so proper to the place and the spectator. The mind naturally loves to lose itself in one of these wildernesses, and to forget the hurry, the noise and splendor of more polished life." [1] Warton also alluded to Thomson in the second volume of his *Essay*. He had been speaking of the fashion of imitating Spenser, and condemning the burlesque and comic style. [2] "To imitate Spenser on a subject that does not partake of the pathos, is not giving a true representation of him. . . . It has been fashionable of late to imitate Spenser, but the likeness of most of the copies, hath consisted rather in using a few of his ancient expressions, than in catching his real manner." He then notes some exceptions, as *The School-mistress*, the *Education of Achilles*, and says, "To these must be added that exquisite piece of wild and romantic imagery, Thomson's Castle of Indolence; the first canto of which, in particular, is marvellously pleasing, and the stanzas have a greater flow and feeling than his blank verse." Shenstone wrote appreciatively of Thomson's poem shortly after it appeared; [3] and his verses to William Lyttleton in 1748, on Thomson's death, speak of the "sweet descriptive bard" in high terms. The service rendered to the English Romantic movement by the *Castle of Indolence* was exceedingly great; Thomson might have done still more work in the same field had his life not been so suddenly cut short.

In 1749 appeared *A Farewell Hymn to the Country, Attempted in the Manner of Spenser's Epithalamion*. This was by the Rev. R. Potter, who was an enthusiastic lover of nature and a great admirer of old English poetry in general, and of Spenser in particular. The *Hymn* was popular, and passed into a second edition the next year. It is not without poetic merit, and has a good musical flow. The stanza in which he alludes to his master may be worth quoting. He has spoken of three poets,

---

[1] *Essay on Pope*, Vol. I., pape 366 (4th ed., 1782).
[2] See Vol. II., page 31.
[3] Letter to Mr. Jago, November 15, 1748.

Milton, Chaucer, and "sweet Cowley," and then proceeds as follows : —

> "And he, forth-beaming thro' the mystic Shade
>     In all the Might of Magic sweetly strong ;
> Who steep'd in Teares the pitious Lines he made,
>     The tendrest Bard that ere empassion'd Song ;
> Or when of Love's Delights he cast to play,
> Couth deftly dight the Lay ;
>     And with gay Girlonds goodly beautifide,
> Bound trew love-wise to grace his bridale Day,
>     With daintie Carrols hymn'd his happy Bride ;
> Lov'd SPENSER, of trew Verse the Well-spring sweet !
> The Footing of whose Feet
>     I, paineful Follower, assay to trace.
> Bring fayrest Floures, the purest Lillies bring,
> With all the purple Pride of all the Spring ;
> And make great Store of Poses trim, to grace
> The Prince of Poets' Race ;
> And Hymen, Hymen, ïo Hymen sing ;
> The Hills, the Dales, the Woods, the Fountaines ring."

In 1751 appeared *The Seasons*, by Moses Mendez (died 1758). Mendez was a Jew, who dabbled in literature. He was famous chiefly for his great wealth, and forms in this respect a curious contrast to the literary beggars of the day. He was the richest poet of his time, leaving a fortune of £100,000 at his death. Mendez was an enthusiastic admirer of Thomson's poetry, and in *The Seasons* he imitated him doubly, by writing on Nature and by adopting the Spenserian stanza. Mendez's poem is divided into four parts, Spring, Summer, Autumn, Winter. He opened with some prefatory stanzas defying the critics, and then goes on as follows : —

> "Ere yet I sing the round-revolving year,
>     And show the toils and pastime of the swain,
> At Alcon's grave I drop a pious tear ;
>     Right well he knew to raise his learned strain,
>     And, like his Milton, scorned the rhiming chain.

> Ah ! cruel fate, to tear him from our eyes ;
>     Receive this wreath, albe the tribute's vain,
> From the green sod may flowers immortal rise,
> To mark the sacred spot where the sweet poet lies."

This reference to Thomson is especially interesting on account of the allusion to blank verse.

Mendez's *Seasons* contains the usual amount of obsolete words, but has in its swing and melody something of the real manner of the master. The fourth stanza in *Spring* shows Mendez at his best : —

> "The balmy cowslip gilds the smiling plain,
>     The virgin snow-drop boasts her silver hue,
> An hundred tints the gaudy daisy stain,
>     And the meek violet, in amis blue,
>     Creeps low to earth, and hides from public view."

Some years later Mendez took the field again, with his *Squire of Dames*. He describes the search of the Squire of Dames for three hundred chaste women, and his ill success. Mendez meant the poem to be both an allegory and a satire. It is in two cantos in the regular Spenserian stanza, and shows how the Squire found every girl unfaithful. At last he goes to the castle of Merlin, and gazes in a magic mirror which will reveal anything asked for. He calls for his own chaste mistress, Columbel, and, to his horror, she and her paramour are represented in a situation which is anything but chaste. At this last straw he swoons and the poem closes.

The *Squire of Dames* shows careful reading of Spenser, and is far above the ordinary imitations. It exhibits great metrical skill ; and some passages are notably Romantic. The description of Merlin's castle is perhaps the most Romantic part of the poem, and, as Mendez's poetry is so little known, I will quote this passage entire : —

" Together now they seek the hermitage
    Deep in the covert of a dusky glade,
Where in his dortour wons the hoary sage.
    The moss-grown trees did form a gloomy shade,
    Their rustling leaves a solemn music made,
And fairies nightly tripped the aweful green,
    And if the tongue of fame hath truth display'd,
Full many a spectre was at midnight seen,
Torn from his earthly grave, a horrid sight! I ween.

Ne rose ne vi'let, glads the cheerless bow'r,
    Ne fringed pink from earth's green bosom grew,
But hemloc dire and every baleful flow'r
    Might here be found, and knots of mystic rue.
    Close to the cell sprong up an auncient yew,
And store of imps were on its boughs ypight,
    At his behests they from its branches flew,
And, in a thousand various forms bedight,
Frisk'd to the moon's pale wain, and revell'd all the night.

Around the cave a clust'ring ivy spread
    In wide embrace his over-twining arms,
Within the walls with characters bespread
    Declar'd the pow'rful force of magic charms,
    Here drugs were plac'd destructive of all harms,
And books that deep futurity could scan ;
    Here stood a spell that of his rage disarms
The mountain lyon till he yields to man ;
With many secrets more which scarce repeat I can." [1]

This is neither moralizing nor smutty; being very different
poetry from either Ridley's *Psyche* or Pitt's *Jordan*. It counts
for something in the history of Romanticism. Mendez illustrates the two-fold nature of the movement, in his love of
Nature, and love of the Past ; and his following Thomson in
both subject and form is note-worthy.

Boyse was not the only vagabond among the Spenserians;
another rascal was the poet Robert Lloyd (1733–1764). He

[1] Canto II., Stanzas 31, 32, 33.

led a terribly dissipated life, was more often drunk than sober
and spent a large portion of the time in prison for debt
He was a professed imitator of Prior, and had a keen and
penetrating wit, which he used unsparingly. In some directions
his tastes seemed to favor the new school. He wrote an
epistle to Garrick, in which he praised the English dramatists,
and Shakspere's departure from Classic rules of art. He
satirized the chorus of the Greek stage.

His remarks on the contemporary craze for imitations are
not bad. He wrote them in 1755 to a friend who was about
to publish a volume of miscellanies. Lloyd warns him against
too much imitation : —

> "Let not your verse, as verse now goes,
>     Be a strange kind of measur'd prose ;
> Nor let your prose, which sure is worse,
>     Want nought but measure to be verse.
> Write from your own imagination,
>     Nor curb your Muse by imitation ;
> For copies show, howe'er exprest,
>     A barren genius at the best.
> — But imitation's all the mode —
>     Yet where one hits, ten miss the road."

He then goes on to complain of the number of Miltonic
imitations, and says : —

> "'Tis by those
> Milton's the model mostly chose
> Who can't write verse, and won't write prose."

His remarks on the Spenserian imitations are interesting : —

> "Others, who aim at fancy, choose
>     To woo the gentle Spenser's muse.
> The poet fixes for his theme
>     An allegory, or a dream.
> Fiction and truth together joins
>     Thro' a long waste of flimsy lines ;

Fondly believes his fancy glows,
And image upon image grows ;
Thinks his strong Muse takes wondrous flights,
Whene'er she sings of peerless wights,
Of dens, of palfreys, spells and knights,
'Till allegory, Spenser's veil,
T' instruct and please in moral tale,
With him 's no veil the truth to shroud,
But one impenetrable cloud."

These octosyllabics are worth quoting, as they show the popularity that Spenserianism had gained. But although Lloyd thus satirized the imitators, he had already joined their ranks. In 1751 he published his *Progress of Envy*. It is a defense of Milton. Lloyd attacks a disreputable Scotchman who had made an onslaught on the reputation of the Puritan poet. Besides the main object of the poem, it is also a panegyric on Spenser, and even Shakspere and Chaucer come in for praise. It is allegorical in form, with the customary number of personified abstractions. The stanza is Spenserian, with nine lines, but with a curious riming scheme.[1]

In 1691 Edmund Smith (1668–1710) made himself somewhat famous by a Latin ode on the death of Dr. Pococke ; in 1751 was published *Thales*, a Spenserian imitation, and apparently a translation of Smith's Latin verses.[2] Who wrote the English stanzas is difficult to ascertain. They are in eight-lines,[3] still another variation on Spenser's original form.

By 1751 Dr. Johnson thought it was about time to speak out. The Spenserians were having things altogether too much their own way, and he was alarmed at such tendencies in the direction of Romanticism. He relieved his mind in the *Rambler*, for May 14, 1751. He says, "the imitation of Spenser . . . by the influence of some men of learning and genius, seems likely to gain upon the age." To imitate Spenser's "fictions and sentiments can incur no reproach,

---

[1] *ab, ab, cd, cd, d.*

[2] The English poem is in Bell's *Fugitive Poetry.*

[3] Riming *abab, b, c, c, c.*

for allegory is perhaps one of the most pleasing vehicles of instruction." So far as Spenser encourages didactic poetry, the doctor naturally thinks he is all right. "But I am very far from extending the same respect to his diction or his stanza. His style was in his own time allowed to be vicious. . . . His stanza is at once difficult and unpleasing; tiresome to the ear by its uniformity, and to the attention by its length." This is a strange criticism coming from an admirer of long poems in the heroic couplet. Johnson closes his paper with one parting shot. "The style of Spenser might by long labour be justly copied; but life is surely given us for higher purposes than to gather what our ancestors have thrown away, and to learn what is of no value, but because it has been forgotten." Dr. Johnson's emphatic protest is the most conclusive evidence as to the strength which the movement had gained by the middle of the century.

In 1754 appeared a very important work — Thomas Warton's *Observations on the Faery Queen*. This had a strong influence in furthering the serious study and appreciation of Spenser. The book will be mentioned again in connection with the critical side of the Romantic movement. Warton made some imitations of his own. Indeed his poetry is wholly imitative, his chief model being Milton, whose ideas and language he borrowed with a free hand. His poems were not published collectively till 1777, but a number of them appeared at occasional intervals. His Spenserian imitations are *Morning*, written in 1745, published 1750, *Elegy on the Death of Frederic, Prince of Wales* (1751), *A Pastoral in the Manner of Spenser* (1753), though there is some doubt as to his authorship of this; and the *Complaint of Cherwell*, written 1761, published 1777. It is curious that with all his knowledge of Spenser, his imitations should not have followed the regular stanza of the *Fairy Queen*.[1] But although he did not pay so close attention

---

[1] The *Elegy* and *Complaint* are six-lined, ending with an Alexandrine, and riming *ab, ab, c, c*. The *Pastoral* is in the same form as the *Shepherd's Calendar* for January and December.

to the form, he was filled with the master's spirit ; allusions to the old poet constantly occur among his verses. In his poem, *The Pleasures of Melancholy*, written in his seventeenth year, he says : —

> " Thro' Pope's soft song tho' all the Graces breathe
> And happiest art adorn his Attic page ;
> Yet does my mind with sweeter transport glow
> As at the root of mossy trunk reclin'd,
> In magic Spenser's wildly-warbled song
> I see deserted Una wander wide
> Thro' wasteful solitudes and lurid heaths."

Thomas Warton, like his brother, was a conscious Romanticist.[1]

Thomas Denton (1724–1777), a minor poet, also belongs to the Spenserian school. He was an Oxford man, receiving his M.A. in 1752. He wrote two imitations of Spenser, *Immortality* (1754) and *The House of Superstition* (1762). Both of these are in ten-lined stanzas, and rime after Prior's model. *Immortality* is imitative of Spenser only in form. Its language is distinctively that of the eighteenth century. It exhibits the contemporary note of melancholy, and the fascination of grave-damp. There are, however, even in this piece some curiously Romantic touches, as in the eleventh stanza, beginning as it unfortunately does, with " Cynthia ": —

> " Pale Cynthia mounted on her silver car
> O'er heaven's blue concave drives her nightly round ;
> See a torn abbey, wrapt in gloom, appear
> Scatter'd in wild confusion o'er the ground.

[1] Some of his general publications are as follows:—
1745. *Five Pastoral Eclogues.*
1747. *Pleasures of Melancholy.*
1749. *Triumph of Isis.*
1751. *Newmarket.*
1754. *Observations*, enlarged in 1762.
1774. First vol., *History of English Poetry*, second vol., 1778, third vol., 1781.
1785. Edition of Milton's *Juvenile Poems.*
1777. Collection of his own poems, second edition, 1778, third, 1779, fourth, 1789.

> Here rav'nous Ruin lifts her wasteful hands
>   O'er briar-grown grots and bramble-shaded graves ;
> Safe from her wrath one weeping marble stands,
>   O'er which the mournful yew its umbrage waves :
> Ope, ope thy pond'rous jaws, thou friendly tomb,
> Close the sad deathful scene, and shroud me in thy womb."

In its general tone the poem, of course, belongs to the school of Blair, Young and Gray.

The *House of Superstition* is a poem in thirteen stanzas, and has a closer resemblance to Spenser than Denton's earlier work, being arranged in allegorical form. It describes the victory of the goddess Truth over the inmates of the castle of Superstition. The poem contains scarcely any obsolete words, and it seems doubtful whether Denton had any first-hand knowledge of Spenser at all. It is more likely that in writing in this form he was simply following the contemporary fashion.

One of these poets who is almost completely forgotten to-day, was Cornelius Arnold (1711–1757 ?). Very little is known of his life. His Spenserian imitation, *The Mirror*, was published as a quarto in 1755, and later in his *Poems* (1757). Arnold had evidently read Shenstone's *School-mistress*, as we learn from his Preface. "The Author begs leave to premise, that in this essay he has retained some few of the old words of Spenser, and adopted the simplicity of the diction in the ludicrous cast, at the end of most of the stanzas, to give it somewhat the exterior air of that great original, however far short he may have fell of the spirit." Arnold's poem contains forty-four regular Spenserian stanzas ; it is a satire on contemporary life and manners, and describes how Death seizes one personage after another, the lawyer, knight, actor, etc. The poetry has not much beauty, but exhibits some originality and considerable force.

In 1756 appeared a very dull poem by Christopher Smart (1722–1770). The *Hymn to the Supreme Being on Recovery from a Dangerous Fit of Illness*, is in six-line stanzas,[1] and is poor stuff. Its form alone makes it necessary to mention it here.

William Wilkie (1721–1772) is connected with the Spenserian school by his poem, *A Dream — In the manner of Spenser*, which appeared in 1759. It was published along with the second edition of the *Epigoniad*, which work gave Wilkie the title of the "Scottish Homer." This was a long epic in nine books, written in the couplet. *A Dream* is a regular Spenserian imitation, containing eighteen stanzas. It is an attack on literary critics — a defense of nature against the canons of the artificial school of criticism. One stanza will suffice to show Wilkie's style: —

> " Though Shakspeare, still disdaining narrow rules,
> His bosom fill'd with Nature's sacred fire,
> Broke all the cobweb limits fix'd by fools,
> And left the world to blame him and admire,
> Yet his reward few mortals would desire ;
> For, of his learned toil, the only meed —
> That ever I could find he did acquire,
> Is that our dull, degenerate, age of lead,
> Says that he wrote by chance, and that he scarce could read."

In 1767 William Junius Mickle (1734–1788) published *The Concubine*, a Spenserian imitation in two cantos. In the second edition (1778) he changed the name, calling it *Sir Martyn*. Although this poem appeared after 1765, and thus strictly carries us beyond the limit of our present study, *The Concubine* deserves a moment's notice, as it had been growing in Mickle's mind for some years. In the Rev. John Sim's *Life of Mickle*, we are told that about his thirteenth year (1746) "Spenser's Faery Queene falling accidentally in his way, he was immediately struck with the picturesque descriptions of that much admired ancient bard, and powerfully incited to imitate his style and manner."[2] In Mickle's preface to his poem — printed with

---

[1] Riming *ab, ab, cc.*     [2] *Mickle's Poetical Works*, London, 1806, page xi.

the second edition in 1778 — he said : " Some reasons, perhaps, may be expected for having adopted the manner of Spenser. To propose a general use of it were indeed highly absurd ; yet it may be presumed there are some subjects on which it may be used with advantage. But not to enter upon any formal defence, the Author will only say, that the fulness and wantonness of description, the quaint simplicity, and above all, the ludicrous, of which the antique phraseology and manner of Spenser are so happily and peculiarly susceptible, inclined him to esteem it not solely as the best, but the only mode of composition adapted to his subject." Here again we have the familiar emphasis laid on the "simplicity," and especially the "ludicrous" element in Spenser.

Mickle's poem is in the regular stanza, and shows considerable familiarity with Spenser ; he adopted both antiquated spelling, and obsolete words, the latter being explained in a Glossary which accompanied the poem.

With this poem we close our view of the Spenserian revival. Editions of Spenser did not keep pace with the growing number of imitations ; it was not until the middle of the century that the demand for Spenser himself became strong. Hughes's edition of 1715 seemed to satisfy the public till 1750, when another edition took the field. This was followed by an edition of the *Fairy Queen* in 1751, and in 1758 three separate editions of the same poem appeared. Another edition of Spenser's *Works* was published in 1778.

Little is needed by way of summary. The imitations began to be numerous after 1736, and the movement reached its climax about 1750. The unconsciousness of the movement is shown by the powerful influence exercised upon it by Pope and Prior. The significant fact that Spenser was by many apprehended only on the ludicrous side, was discussed at some length in the early part of this chapter.[1]

---

[1] See *Appendix* for a list of Spenserian imitations.

# CHAPTER V.

## THE INFLUENCE OF MILTON IN THE ROMANTIC MOVEMENT. — THE LITERATURE OF MELANCHOLY.

WE do not to-day think of Milton primarily as a Romantic poet; his great epic would more naturally place him in the ranks of the Classicists; and his remarkable devotion to the study of Greek and Latin authors, with the powerful influence they had upon him, would seem to separate him widely from Romanticism. To the men of the eighteenth century, however, his message was Romantic. He was shunned and practically neglected by the Augustans, whose Classicism was so thoroughly Horatian; and those who admired him did so more on account of the bulk of his epic and its theological theme, than from a genuine love and appreciation of his poetry. The young Romanticists claimed Milton for their own; his name was a rallying cry; and they followed him in thought, language, and versification. His influence cannot be traced out in detail so clearly as Spenser's; but it was a quickening force, as any one who reads eighteenth century minor poetry may see for himself. I have already spoken of his influence on the Reaction in Form; his blank verse was steadily imitated and did much toward dethroning the couplet; his octosyllabics were still more effective, and his sonnets leavened English poetry after 1750. But it was not so much in *form* as in *thought* that Milton affected the Romantic movement; and although *Paradise Lost* was always reverentially considered his greatest work, it was not at this time nearly so effective as his minor poetry; and in the latter it was *Il Penseroso* — the love of meditative comfortable melancholy — that penetrated most deeply into the Romantic soul. Even such a poem as Dyer's *Fleece*, although in blank verse, is more reminiscent of the juvenile poems than

of the epics ; and the blank verse of the Warton brothers is
charged with the sentiments and phrases of Milton's octosyllabics.    The influence of Milton cannot, accordingly, be seen in
so distinct a literary fashion as the Spenserian fad ; it must be
traced in a different way, and along more general lines.

It was in the *Spectator* for December 31, 1711, that Addison
announced his intention of writing a series of papers on Milton ;
but important as Addison's work was, he was not the first man
to bring Milton into public notice.    Editions of Milton had
been regularly supplying a quiet but steady demand.

The well-known men who show the influence of Milton most
clearly are the Warton brothers, Collins, Mason, and Gray.
But there were many lesser lights who give evidence of close
study of the Puritan poet.    For example, William Hamilton of
Bangour imitated Milton in his octosyllabic poem *Contemplation*.[1]
He shows this perhaps most clearly in his fondness for Ab-
stractions ; and indeed the subsequent fashion of personifying
Abstractions — though dating back even much earlier than the
Morality Plays — seems in the new Romantic movement to
have flowed largely from Milton.    Consider these lines from
Hamilton's poem : —

> " Anger, with wild disorder'd face ;
> And Malice pale of famish'd face ;
> Loud-tongued Clamour, get thee far
> Hence, to wrangle at the bar ;
> With opening mouths vain Rumour hung ;
> And falsehood with her serpent tongue ;
> Revenge, her blood-shot eyes on fire,
> And hissing Envy's snaky tire ;
> With Jealousy, the fiend most fell,
> Who bears about his inmate hell,
> Now far apart with haggard mien
> To lone Suspicion list'ning seen," etc.[2]

This kind of thing became extremely common.

[1] Written in or before 1739.
[2] Observe the similarity of all this to Collins's Ode on the *Passions*.

Joseph Warton (1722–1800) is one of the most important names in the history of English Romanticism.[1]

From the start his sympathy was wholly with the new movement. He sprang enthusiastically into the ranks, burning his bridges in the most reckless manner. In his prose writings he showed himself to be what few men were at that time — a Romanticist, not by accident, but with malice aforethought.

In this chapter, however, we are concerned not with his prose, but with his poetry, which sounded some of the earliest and most distinct Romantic tones. He was a follower of Milton, and his poetry is in the *Il Penseroso* mood ; the fondness for solitude and twilight, for personal subjective communion with Nature — these common Romantic qualities are strikingly characteristic of Warton's poetry. From 1740 to 1760 English literature is full of the still music of sentimental melancholy, with a burden of Dead Marches. In 1740, when only eighteen, Joseph Warton wrote *The Enthusiast; or the Lover of Nature,* a poem in blank verse. It is in the minor key, full of Romantic feeling, and vibrating with Miltonic echoes. The youth gave vent to his feelings as follows : —

> " Rich in her weeping country's spoils, Versailles
> May boast a thousand fountains, that can cast
> The tortur'd waters to the distant Heavn's ;
> Yet let me choose some pine-topt precipice
> Abrupt and shaggy, whence a foamy stream,
> Like Arno, tumbling roars ;  or some black heath,
> Where straggling stands the mournful Juniper,
> Or yew-tree scath'd."

1 Dates of his chief publications:
> 1740. *The Enthusiast* (written ; I think not published till 1744).
> 1746. *Odes.*
> 1749. *Ode to Mr. West.*
> 1749–53. Edition of Vergil.
> 1756. *Essay on Pope* — second volume in 1782.
> 1797. Edition of Pope.
> 1799. Edition of Dryden.

Again we have touches akin to Rousseau's "back-to-nature" sentiment : —

> "Happy the first of men, ere yet confin'd
> To smoky cities ; who in sheltering groves,
> Warm caves and deep-sunk vallies, liv'd and lov'd,
> By cares unwounded."

His comparison of Addison with Shakspere shows the defiant feeling of rebellion, which made the Wartons the true leaders of the Romantic reaction: —

> "What are the lays of artful Addison,
> Coldly correct, to Shakespear's warblings wild?
> Whom on the winding Avon's willow'd banks
> Fair Fancy found, and bore the smiling babe
> To a close cavern." [1]

The poem concludes with a passionate cry for solitude and wild nature. Milton and Thomson were Warton's masters in this poem ; it is a remarkable production for a youth of eighteen, not only in its intrinsic merit, but in its prophetic insight of what was coming. *The Enthusiast* is certainly one of the most important poems in the Romantic movement.

In December, 1746, Joseph Warton published a thin volume of Odes. His advertisement has some significant remarks. He says : "The Public has been so much accustomed of late to didactic poetry alone, and essays on moral subjects, that any work where the imagination is much indulged, will perhaps not be relished or regarded. The author therefore of these pieces is in some pain lest certain austere critics should think them too fanciful or descriptive. But as he is convinced that the fashion of moralizing in verse has been carried too far, and as he looks upon Invention and imagination to be the chief faculties of a poet, so he will be happy if the following Odes

---

[1] Reminiscent, of course, of Milton's calling Shakspere "Fancy's child," and "Warble his native wood-notes wild." Observe also the studied alliteration of this passage from Warton.

may be looked upon as an attempt to bring back Poetry into its right channel."

This is a rap over the knuckles for Classicism; in a crude and rough way Warton here articulated the Romantic doctrine. He had believed all this in 1740, and during his whole life he clung to these views with singular tenacity.

This small volume contained fourteen odes, in various metres. Some of the subjects will give an idea of the character of the book — Fancy, Liberty, Health, Superstition, Evening, The Nightingale, Solitude, etc. The Ode to Fancy is full of echoes of Milton: —

> " Haste Fancy from the scenes of folly,
> To meet the matron Melancholy,
> Goddess of the tearful eye,
> That loves to fold her arms and sigh ;
> Let us with silent footsteps go
> To charnels and the house of woe,
> To Gothic churches, vaults and tombs
> Where each sad night some virgin comes,
> With throbbing breast, and faded cheek,
> Her promis'd bridegroom's urn to seek."

This is an excellent example of what is meant by the "literature of melancholy," and of course its original inspiration from *Il Penseroso* is indisputable. In the same ode appears an allusion to Shakspere, where Warton is again thinking of Milton's expression, "Fancy's child." [1] Milton's casual remark that Shakspere was the child of Fancy seemed to produce a profound impression on the Romanticists.

The *Ode to Health*, written on his recovery from the small-pox, is noteworthy for the opinion expressed of Milton in the last stanza : —

[1] " O hear our prayer, O hither come
From thy lamented Shakespear's tomb,
On which thou lov'st to sit at eve,
Musing o'er thy darling's grave."

> " Where Maro and Musaeus sit
>     Listening to Milton's loftier song,
> With sacred silent wonder smit,
>     While, monarch of the tuneful throng,
> Homer in rapture throws his trumpet down,
> And to the Briton gives his amyranthine crown."

Homer, and especially Vergil, doing homage to Milton would certainly have been a sacrilegious thought to Augustan minds. For Dryden's famous lines were considered simply as the hyperbole of complimentary verses.

The *Ode to Evening* has some passages which instantly suggest Gray's *Elegy.* For example :—

> " Hail, meek-eyed maiden, clad in sober grey,
>     Whose soft approach the weary woodman loves,
>     As, homeward bent to kiss his prattling babes,
>     He jocund whistles thro' the twilight groves."

And another stanza has the line :—

> " And with hoarse hummings of unnumber'd flies."

The *Ode to Solitude* fitly closes this remarkable collection of poetry. This ode is strictly Romantic in tone, and with the other thirteen stands as one of the finger-posts of the whole Romantic movement.

Warton's *Ode to West* (1749), on the latter's translation of *Pindar*, gives, especially in the third stanza, his contemptuous opinion of Augustan verse.[1]

What Warton laid down as principles in his prose essays, he tried to exemplify in his verse. He turned directly away from Classicism, and drew his inspiration from fresh out-door nature and from meditative melancholy. Perhaps he is the first *consciously* Romantic poet in the eighteenth century. Mr. Courthope says of Warton's *Enthusiast:* " It may certainly be regarded as the starting-point of the romantic revival, as it expresses all that love of solitude and that yearning for the

---

[1] The stanza begins:

> "Away, enervate bards, away,
>     Who spin the courtly, silken lay,"

spirit of a by-gone age, which are especially associated with the genius of the romantic school of poetry." [1] The poem can hardly be regarded as the starting-point, as I have shown in these pages that the spirit of Romanticism had appeared in some strength earlier than 1740 ; but Warton's peculiar distinction is that he was a Romanticist with a program.

Thomas Warton (1728–1790) was even a more direct follower of Milton than his older brother. The two men were from the start avowed Romanticists, both writing Romantic poetry, and Joseph helping the movement by destructive criticism of Pope, while Thomas assisted by favorable criticism of Spenser. T. Warton's poems are so patched with Miltonic phrases, that when the quotations are removed scarcely anything remains. With his intense Romantic feeling it is singular that he should also have written one long imitation of Pope — the heavy satire *Newmarket* (1751). In 1745, while still a boy, he wrote and in 1747 published *The Pleasures of Melancholy*. The title was of course suggested by Akenside's *Pleasures of Imagination*, in the wake of which followed "Pleasures" of all kinds. In composition T. Warton had no more originality than his brother, but he came out positively for Romanticism and his *Pleasures of Melancholy* is really a companion-piece to the *Enthusiast*. The influence of Milton also appears as plainly : —

> "Beneath yon ruin'd abbey's moss-grown piles
>   Oft let me sit, at twilight hour of eve,
>   Where thro' some western window the pale Moon
>   Pours her long-levell'd rule of streaming light ;
>   While sullen sacred silence reigns around,
>     Save the lone screech-owl's note,[2] who builds his bow'r
>   Amid the mould'ring caverns dark and damp,
>   Or the calm breeze, that rustles in the leaves
>   Of flaunting ivy, that with mantle green
>     Invests some wasted tow'r."

[1] *Pope's Works*, Vol. V., page 365.
[2] The screech-owl was a stock figure in the "Literature of Melancholy."

He also compares the artificiality of court life with the happiness of romantic solitude.

His ode on the *Approach of Summer* is a close imitation of Milton. A specimen will show how freely Warton borrowed:—

> "Haste thee, nymph ! and hand in hand,
>  With thee lead a buxom band ;
>  Bring fantastic-footed Joy,
>  With Sport, that yellow-tressed boy."

One of the most strictly Romantic passages in this poem is as follows :—

> "Yet still the sultry noon t' appease
>  Some more romantic scene might please ;
>  Or fairy bank, or magic lawn,
>  By Spenser's lavish pencil drawn ;
>
> .    .    .    .    .    .    .
>
>  On that hoar hill's aerial light,
>  In solemn state, where waving wide,
>  Thick pines with darkening umbrage hide
>  The rugged vaults and riven tow'rs
>  Of that proud castle's painted bow'rs
>  Whence Hardy Knute, a baron bold,
>  In Scotland's martial days of old,
>  Descended from the stately feast,
>  Begirt with many a warrior guest."

The Romanticists particularly delighted in "umbrage"— thick woods, ruined castle-towers, twilight coloring and all quietistic landscape scenery.

Two of T. Warton's odes are on distinctly Romantic subjects —*The Crusade* and the *Grave of King Arthur*— published in 1777. They were both in octosyllabics. His nine sonnets were all on the Miltonic model, and the three on Stonehenge, King Arthur's Round Table, and the river Lodon, are full of the spirit of Romanticism. The very word "romantic" was a favorite with T. Warton ; he constantly uses it in both poetry and prose.

A critical estimate of the poetry of the Warton brothers would find in it much imitation and little immortality; but its historical significance is hard to overestimate. They followed models, but their models were Romantic and decidedly anti-Classical.

The best lyrical poet of the time was William Collins (1721–1759). In one sense of the word Collins was thoroughly classical; in his verses we find the perfect finish and grace of Greek form. In sentiment, however, he was with the young Romanticists, and was strongly influenced by Milton. It is going a little too far to say that "his poetry was the first distinct utterance of the school which uttered in Warton's essay a public protest against the canons accepted by Pope and his followers," [1] but he certainly played a part in the movement. Like many of the Romanticists, Collins began to write poetry in early youth; while a boy at school he published some verses to a lady.[2] In the *Gentleman's Magazine* for October, 1739, appeared three poems — written by Collins, J. Warton his school-mate, and a third friend. In January, 1742, appeared his *Persian Eclogues*.[3] In this enterprise Collins pretended to be only a translator. In the Preface he apologized for the "rich and figurative" style of the Persians. He also spoke of their "elegancy and wildness of thought," saying, "our genius's are . . . much too cold for the entertainment of such sentiments." After reading this Preface, one expects to find verses rather startling; but the four eclogues are really in no way remarkable either for literary merit or for Romantic feeling; and they are written in the heroic couplet. In December, 1746,[4] he published a few days after the appearance of J. Warton's *Odes*, his *Odes on Several Descriptive and Allegoric*

---

1 Stephen's *Dictionary of National Biography.*

2 *Gentleman's Magazine,* January, 1739.

3 Afterward (edition 1757) called *Oriental Eclogues.*

4 First edition is dated 1747; but it was really published in December, 1746. Gray's letter on the odes of Warton and Collins is very interesting. (See his *Works,* ed. Gosse, II., page 160.)

*Subjects.* The two friends had intended to publish their Odes together in one volume, but curiously enough Dodsley wouldn't take Collins's verses; and still more curiously, the immediate result seemed to prove Dodsley's judgment entirely correct; for Warton's book was successful, while Collins's attracted very little attention.[1] This little, neglected volume contained twelve odes, among them some pieces which are to-day known everywhere. Collins was a great admirer of Shakspere and Spenser, and though his love for Milton was not so strongly avowed, it appears in his great fondness for personified abstractions, and in occasional phrases.[2] His beautiful *Ode to Evening* is wholly Romantic in mood, and the last part of his *Ode on the Poetical Character* has the Romantic flavor. His *Ode on the Death of Thomson* (June, 1749) showed a true appreciation of the poet of nature. His *Ode to Simplicity* (1746) is in the form which Milton used for his Christmas hymn.

The most significant poem of Collins — his Ode on the Scottish Superstitions — will be considered later in another connection. Collins was steadily gravitating in the direction of Romanticism, and had his health lasted, he might have played an important part in the movement. Judging by actual results, he does not count for anything like so much in the history of Romanticism as the Warton brothers, although his poetry is immeasurably superior in literary excellence.

The poetry of Gray demands a separate chapter; he was influenced, more perhaps than he himself thought, by Milton. His *Elegy* was the culmination of the literature of melancholy, as well as of the Church-yard school. In its pensive mood and love of twilight it is in the regular *Il Penseroso* vein; in its meditation on death and the grave, it belongs more properly to the school of Blair and Young.

---

[1] J. Warton was really one of the first men to recognize Collins's lyrical power. (See his *Essay on Pope*, Vol. I., page 69.)

[2] Such as in the *Ode to Liberty*.
              " Play with the tangles of her hair."

It is rather difficult to classify the poet William Mason (1725–1797), except to say that he was first, last, and all the time an imitator. Mason's character, while not vicious, is repelling because of his enormous conceit. It seems strange that a man of his offensiveness should have been so long the intimate friend of gentlemen so fastidious as Gray and Walpole. Gray treated Mason like an affectionate hound, and after Gray's death Walpole seems to have continued friendly to Mason simply because of the opportunities it gave him to talk about Gray. Walpole's constant affection and reverence for Gray's memory are exceedingly beautiful. Gray corresponded considerably with Mason, but one feels that both men were conscious of the former's intellectual superiority. Gray shows it by a mild contempt only half concealed ; and Mason shows it in his usual fawning style. No man ever came into close contact with Gray without being impressed by the loftiness of his character and his strong intellectuality ; but Mason, while giving the first rank to the Cambridge recluse, undoubtedly felt that with this one exception he himself was the poet of the age. His connection with Gray, and the fact that he edited Gray's literary remains have kept Mason alive ; his poetry is not altogether without merit, but it "smells of mortality." Lowell said that Gray and Mason together could not make the latter a poet.

Mason's *Musaeus* (1747), a poem in imitation of Milton's *Lycidas*, has been already alluded to ; Milton speaks in this poem in blank verse, although Milton bewailing the death of Pope is not very easy to imagine, either from the literary or theological point of view. Mason's sonnets also show Milton's influence ; intrinsically they are of little value. His *Il Pacifico* and *Il Bellicoso* [1] were perhaps as direct imitations of Milton's juvenile poetry as the whole movement produced ; though there were so many minor versifiers that it is dangerous to

---

[1] *Il Bellicoso* and *Il Pacifico* were written a year or two before 1747 ; the latter was first published in 1748, on the conclusion of the peace of Aix-la-Chapelle.

make sweeping statements.[1]   Mason dabbled to some extent in Romanticism, especially after he came under Gray's influence. He wrote two tragedies, *Elfrida* (1751) and *Caractacus* (1759). These are on the model of the ancient Greek drama, and though they contain some fine passages, they lack vitality. In some letters published with *Elfrida* Mason gave his theories of dramatic art.   They can hardly be called Romantic, as he stoutly upholds the Unities and insists on the retention of the Chorus.   He was willing, however, to modify the severity of Greek taste so far as concerned subject-matter, and pleaded for the introduction of bits of nature-description.   He said : "I meant only to pursue the antient method, so far as it is probable a Greek poet, were he alive, would now do, in order to adapt himself to the genius of our times, and the character of our Tragedy. . . . for the sake of natural embellishment, and to reconcile mere modern readers to that simplicity of fable, in which I thought it necessary to copy the Antients, I contrived to lay the scene in an old romantic forest."[2]

The subject-matter of Mason's dramas, with all their iciness of treatment, is really Romantic.   *Caractacus* is a story of Druid times, in which Druids play an important part; the scene is laid in Mona.   The virtuous maiden and brave youthful hero are, of course, sufficiently prominent; but there are some passages that may be called strictly Romantic.   They show Gray's influence.   Thus : —

> " Mona on Snowdon calls :
>     Hear, thou King of mountains, hear ;
>     Hark, she speaks from all her strings ;
>     Hark, her loudest echo rings ;
>     King of mountains, bend thine ear ;
>     Send thy spirits, send them soon,
>     Now, when Midnight and the Moon
>     Meet upon thy front of snow ;
>         \*      \*      \*      \*      \*

[1] For example, another imitation equally close was *L'Amoroso*, by the " Rev. Mr. P." See *Bell's Fugitive Poetry*, Vol. XI.

[2] Letter I.; in his *Works* (1764).

Snowdon has heard the strain ;
Hark, amid the wond'ring grove
Other harpings answer clear,
Other voices meet our ear,

\*     \*     \*     \*     \*

Rustling vestments brush the ground ;
Round, and round, and round they go,
Thro' the twilight, thro' the shade,
Mount the oak's majestic head,
And gild the tufted mistletoe." [1]

Mason also translated from P. H. Mallet a " Runic " poem, thus touching Romanticism on the side where Gray and Percy were chiefly interested. Mason was often coupled with Gray by contemporary critics, and the alleged obscurity of their odes was freely satirized.

Among the imitators of Milton, only a few names have been mentioned ; the subject is too vague and elusive to warrant a rehearsal of the long list of poetasters who show his influence. Many of the Spenserians greatly admired Milton, and imitated him along with the Elizabethan poet.

Vibrating with the literature of melancholy, which was so distinct a note in Romanticism, there was a still deeper undertone in the poetry of the grave-yard, and in long reflective verses on death and immortality. This strange growth will receive only a passing notice. It was not exactly Romantic, though akin to the Romantic feeling, and was certainly reactionary to the Augustan spirit, which strove to taboo both the shadow of the grave and the mystery of the future. This tolling-bell in literature seemed to the new school to give a " pleasing gloom," and had perhaps its most conspicuous example in Young, who stimulated his fancy by composing under the light of a candle stuck in a skull. All this movement was more preparatory to Romanticism than actually a part of it. The tones of despair, the odor of the charnel-house,

[1] *Works*, page 196.

the world-old meditation on the shortness of life and the ce
tainty of death — the new emphasis laid on all this evidentl
contained seeds of the Romantic movement. The Church-yard
school began with Parnell's *Night-Piece on Death*, in the earl
years of the century. Blair's *Grave* (1743) and Young's *Nigh
Thoughts* (1742–45) and Gray's *Elegy* (1751) were the principa
contributions to permanent literature that the school produce
Blair and Young, apart from their versification, touch Romant
cism only on this side — the joy of gloom, the fondness fo
bathing one's temples in the dank night air and the musica
delight of the screech-owl's shriek. Mr. Perry says Young
had much of the "crude ore of Romanticism," and Mr. Gosse
speaks of his "note of romantic despair." [1]

The elegiac quatrain, a form of versification naturally suited
to the literature of melancholy, became very popular about th
middle of the century. Shenstone was very fond of the elegy
and wrote an interesting essay on the subject, in which h
spoke of the aim of poetry, discussed different styles of versifi
cation, etc. Shenstone himself composed a large number o
elegies, but in Gray's celebrated poem the elegy rose to it
highest perfection. Gray made it exceedingly fashionable, anc
swarms of imitations of his church-yard poem poured from the
press.[2] Its influence was felt immediately, not only in England.
but all over Europe. Mr. Gosse says, "the Elegy has exercised an influence on all the poetry of Europe, from Denmark
to Italy, from France to Russia. With the exception of certain

---

[1] These four lines in *Night Thoughts* may have suggested to Goldsmith an idea
for his famous passage in *The Deserted Village* : —

> " As some tall tow'r, or lofty mountain's brow,
>     Detains the sun, illustrious from its height ;
>     While rising vapours and descending shades
>     With damps, and darkness, drown the spacious vale."

[2] Gray's *Elegy* was published February 16, 1751, and went through four editions i
two months. Then came editions in rapid succession, eleven in all. It was once more
printed in 1753, and in that form had a second edition. It also appeared in Dodsley's
*Miscellany*, and was largely pirated.

works of Byron and Shakespeare, no English poem has been so widely admired and imitated abroad." [1]

The church-yard school lasted for many years. The aspirants for prizes in the universities chose as subjects "Death," "The Grave," "Immortality," etc.[2] Even as late as 1787, Mason wrote an elegy, *In a Church-yard in South Wales.*

The literature of melancholy must certainly be considered an important factor in the beginnings of Romanticism. In its subjective tone, in its vague aspiration, fondness for solitude and gloomy meditation, it was quite different from the tone of Augustan literature; and its master was none other than Milton.

[1] *Life of Gray*, page 97.
[2] For example, Porteus's prize poem in 1759: *Death ; a Poetical Essay.*

# CHAPTER VI.

## REVIVAL OF THE PAST. — GOTHICISM AND CHIVALRY.

I shall give only the briefest notice of the revival of Gothic tastes and of the renewed interest in Chivalry. It is well known that in the course of the eighteenth century public taste in these matters suffered a complete revolution; for in the last decade Gothicism and Chivalry were as popular as they had been unpopular during the reign of Pope. I propose in this chapter to point out the evidences of the transition — to trace the beginnings of the new fashion. It is to this part of the development of Romanticism that Walter Scott belongs, and of which he was perhaps the culmination. We may conveniently call this the *objective* side of the movement, as distinguished from the *subjective*, which advanced parallel with it. The former pertains to the subject-matter; the latter to the mood of the author, as we say that Scott was Romantic because of his subjects and Byron because of his sentimental mood. Both aspects are equally important in English Romanticism, but the objective side reached its fullest development later. For the present we are thus concerned only with signs of the revival of interest in what was " Gothic " — as it affected architecture, literature, and the study of the military aspect of mediæval life.

Everyone knows how low the word " Gothic " had sunk in the Augustan age. In the pages of Addison and Pope, the term " Gothic " was, of course, one of reproach and contempt, whether applied to architecture or to poetry. It was not until after 1750 that Gothicism showed any signs of coming again into favor. " If in the history of British art," says Eastlake, "there is one period more distinguished than another for its neglect of Gothic, it was certainly the middle of the eighteenth century." But "an author . . . appeared to whose writings and to whose influence as an admirer of Gothic art we believe may be ascribed one of the chief causes which induced its present revival." Of course Eastlake refers to Horace Walpole (1717–1797). "It is impossible to peruse either the letters or the romances of this remarkable man without being struck by the unmistakable evidence which they contain of his Mediæval predilections. . . . The position which he occupies with regard to art resembles in many respects that in which he stands as a man of letters. His labours were not profound in either field. But their result was presented to the public in a form which gained him rapid popularity both as an author and a *dilettante*. As a collector of curiosities he was probably influenced more by a love of old world associations than by any sound appreciation of artistic design."[1]

These words are a sufficiently accurate and concise description of Walpole's influence on the Gothic revival. Walpole was not a sincere and philosophical Romanticist, nor did he ever claim to be such. He was a gentleman who dabbled in art and literature and took up Gothicism as a new fad; his Romanticism was largely due to the powerful influence of his friend Gray. But without any conscious attempt at revolutionary leadership, his influence on the Romantic movement was undoubtedly great. He made himself felt in two ways.

1. He made Gothicism fashionable by his home and collections at Strawberry Hill.

2. His *Castle of Otranto* was the pioneer of a long succession of Gothic romances.

Walpole's taste for the picturesque appears as early as Gray's, though his appreciation was not so keen nor his emotion so deep. Walpole as well as Gray described the Grande Chartreuse excursion. "But the road, West, the road !

---

[1] *History of the Gothic Revival*, page 42 *et seq.*

winding round a prodigious mountain, and surrounded with others, all shagged with hanging woods, obscured with pines, or lost in clouds! Below, a torrent breaking through cliffs, and tumbling through fragments of rocks! Sheets of cascades forcing their silver speed down channelled precipices, and hasting into the roughened river at the bottom! Now and then an old foot-bridge, with a broken rail, a leaning cross, a cottage, or the ruin of an hermitage! This sounds too bombast and too romantic to one that has not seen it, too cold for one that has." [1]

It was about 1750 that Walpole began to erect the building afterward so famous as Strawberry Hill. He wrote to Sir Horace Mann, January 10, 1750, " I am going to build a little gothic castle at Strawberry Hill." After this date his letters contain many references to the " castle " and to "gothic" things in general. In another letter to Mann, February 25, 1750, he explained and defended his tastes. " I shall speak much more gently to you, my dear child, though you don't like Gothic architecture. The Grecian is only proper for magnificent and public buildings. Columns and all their beautiful ornaments, look ridiculous when crowded into a closet or a cheese-cake house. The variety is little, and admits no charming irregularities. I am almost as fond of the Sharawaggi, or Chinese want of symmetry, in buildings, as in grounds or gardens. I am sure, whenever you come to England, you will be pleased with the liberty of taste into which we are struck, and of which you can have no idea ! " The public taste in buildings and in laying out grounds had indeed changed ; and the change was symptomatic of the whole Romantic movement. English gardens about this time were relieved of the artificial, regularly cut paths and hedges, and were made more and more to take on the appearance of wild nature.

If some middle-class wealthy Englishman had for his own amusement built such a Gothic castle as the one called

[1] Letter to Richard West, September 30, 1739.

Strawberry Hill, he would probably have been greeted only with ridicule. But when Horace Walpole, the glass of fashion and the mould of form, drew attention to his new-fangled architecture, he carried London society with him. The fame of Strawberry Hill and its curiosities grew apace ; and though the real similarity of the building to Gothic architecture would to-day count for nothing, its effect in re-awakening the study and love of Gothicism counted for much in the middle of the eighteenth century. The impulse that Walpole gave to the Gothic revival on its architectural side was probably greater than that of any other man. Professor Beers remarks that mediæval *architecture* had a decided advantage in England over other forms of mediæval art ; for the latter were known only to a few scholars, whereas the architecture was known to all in such buildings as the Tower of London, Westminster Abbey, Lichfield and Salisbury Cathedrals, and other places. By calling public attention to mediæval buildings that were in advanced stages of decay, Walpole preserved them from complete destruction. Before this time people had not thought them worthy of especial admiration. They were used for all sorts of ignominious purposes.

The craze for Gothic architecture that followed the "gingerbread" castle at Strawberry Hill had a strong side-influence on the revival of the Romantic spirit in literature. Architecture and literature are intimately connected, there being something of the same difference between Greek and Gothic architecture that exists between Classic and Romantic poetry. In fact, it was Walpole's taste in architecture that led directly to his second great service to the Romantic movement, his *Castle of Otranto*. His own literary taste was not Romantic, as will presently appear ; the same whim that created Strawberry Hill gave birth to his Gothic romance.

Walpole had not the slightest idea of revolutionizing public literary taste by the *Castle of Otranto*. His well-known description of the origin of this book is given in two letters

to the Rev. W. Cole.   Writing February 28, 1765, he says,
"Though we love the same ages, you must excuse worldly
me for preferring the romantic scenes of antiquity.   If you
will tell me how to send it, and are partial enough to me to
read a profane work in the style of former centuries, I shall
convey to you a little story-book, which I published some
time ago, though not boldly with my own name ; but it has
succeeded so well, that I do not any longer *entirely* keep the
secret.   Does the title, 'The Castle of Otranto,' tempt you?"
Again, writing March 9, 1765 : — "Your partiality to me and
Strawberry have, I hope, inclined you to excuse the wildness
of the story. . . .   Shall I ever confess to you, what was the
origin of this romance ?   I waked one morning, in the beginning
of last June, from a dream, of which all I could recover was,
that I had thought myself in an ancient castle (a very natural
dream for a head like mine filled with Gothic story) and that
on the uppermost bannister of a great staircase I saw a
gigantic hand in armour.   In the evening I sat down, and
began to write, without knowing in the least what I intended
to say or relate.   The work grew on my hands, and I grew
fond of it. . . .   In short, I was . . . engrossed with my tale,
which I completed in less than two months."

It was in June, 1764, that Walpole began his story, and he
completed it August 6.   It was published December 24 of the
same year.   In the preface he gave a fictitious account of the
romance, saying that he had found the work in the library of
an ancient Catholic family in the North of England.   " It was
printed at Naples, in the black letter, in the year 1529. . . .
Some apology for it is necessary.   Miracles, visions, necro-
mancy, dreams, and other preternatural events, are exploded
now, even from romances.   That was not the case when our
author wrote. . . . Belief in every kind of prodigy was . . .
established in those dark ages."

In the preface to the second edition Walpole begged the
public's pardon for pretending that the book was a translation.

" It was an attempt," he said, " to blend the two kinds of romance, the ancient and the modern. In the former, all was imagination and improbability ; in the latter, nature is always intended to be, and sometimes has been, copied with success. Invention has not been wanting ; but the great resources of fancy have been dammed up, by a strict adherence to common life." The remainder of the preface is occupied with a defense of Shakspere, who had been attacked by Voltaire for mingling the comic with the tragic in his plays.

Walpole had misgivings about the "wildness" of the story, and rather expected an outburst of critical denunciation. Writing to M. Elie de Beaumont, March 18, 1765, he said, " How will you be surprised to find a narrative of the most improbable and absurd adventures ! How will you be amazed to hear that a country of whose good sense you have an opinion should have applauded so wild a tale ! But you must remember, Sir, that whatever good sense we have, we are not yet in any light chained down to precepts and inviolable laws. All that Aristotle or his superior commentators, your authors, have taught us, has not yet subdued us to regularity ; we still prefer the extravagant beauties of Shakspeare and Milton to the cold and well-disciplined merit of Addison and even to the sober and correct march of Pope." It must be remembered that in this passage Walpole is describing the taste of the English people rather than his own preferences ; and his remarks show that the new critical school in England, represented by the Wartons, Young, and others, was making itself deeply felt.

Walpole was surprised at the success of the *Castle of Otranto.* The whole impression was sold in less than three months. Writing to the Earl of Hertford, March 26, 1765, he says, " The success . . . has, at last, brought me to own it, though the wildness of it made me terribly afraid ; but it was comfortable to have it please so much, before any mortal suspected the author ; indeed, it met with too much

honour far, for at first it was universally believed to be Mr.
Gray's."

Mason had been completely duped by Walpole's first preface,
and said that no man of the time had "imagination enough to
invent such a story." Even Gray liked it, his Romanticism
getting the better of his critical faculty. He wrote to Walpole,
December 30, 1764, " It engages our attention here, makes
some of us cry a little, and all in general afraid to go to bed
o' nights." Walpole had shown his manuscript to Gray, and
the latter had recommended publication.

To-day it is impossible for us to take the *Castle of Otranto*
seriously ; to us it is ridiculous and bathetic.[1] But in 1764 it
was a kind of revelation, and its immense popularity shows
how hungrily the people devoured Romantic food. It was the
pioneer of all the wild tales of blood and ghosts that followed
its appearance, and thus, in some sense, it was an epoch-
making book. Clara Reeve's *Old English Baron* professedly
imitated in its general manner Walpole's story, and the works of
Mrs. Radcliffe (1764–1823) are in the direct line of succession.

The modern romances of chivalry, however, cannot be
truthfully said to have *originated* with Walpole, although his
book gave the movement its greatest impetus. In 1762 was
published *Longsword; an Historical Romance.* The title-page
omits the writer's name, but the real author was the Rev.
Thomas Leland, D.D. (1722–1785). He was a learned divine,
born in Dublin, who afterwards achieved fame in the Ossianic
controversy. *Longsword,* though never read nowadays, has

---

[1] The scene from the story which is always selected for especial ridicule is where
" three drops of blood fell from the nose of Alfonso's statue " (Chapter IV.). But
this idea did not originate with Walpole; it seems to have been regarded as simply
an evil omen, and did not appear then in a ludicrous light. In Dryden's play
*Amboyna* (1673), Act IV., Scene I., I ran across the following passage, and doubtless
much earlier allusions can be found in ballads: —

> " Something within me does forbode me ill;
> I stumbled when I enter'd first this Wood;
> My Nostrils bled three Drops; then stop'd the Blood,
> And not one more wou'd follow."

deep significance, for it points directly to Scott. In the Advertisement the author said : "The outlines of the following story, and some of the incidents and more minute circumstances, are to be found in the antient English historians." That is, Leland took his plot after the fashion of the Elizabethan playwrights. The brave youth and aggressively virtuous maiden figure conspicuously in this book, as they did in Walpole and in the later romances. One quotation will suffice to show the style of *Longsword:* — "A youth who seemed just rising to manhood, of graceful form, tall of stature, and with limbs of perfect shape, lay sorely wounded upon the ground, languid, pale, and bloody. Over him hung one in the habit of a page, younger, and still more exquisitely beautiful, piercing the air with lamentations, and eagerly employed in binding up the wounds of the fallen youth, with locks of comely auburn, torn from a fair though dishevelled head."[1] No more of this, for Goddes dignite !

*Longsword* is tedious to read, but interesting on account of its early date — two years before the *Castle of Otranto.* The two stories have some points of resemblance, although one is a historical and the other a Gothic romance. But *Longsword* is more of a forerunner of Scott than the other ; it is a romance of the days of Henry III. and is crammed full of the adventures of chivalry. It is also worth notice that the primary object of *Longsword* was not to instruct, but to amuse.[2] Clara Reeve (1738–1803), in her *Progress of Romance* (1785), has in one of the dialogues the following interesting reference to *Longsword.*[3] Euphanasia mentions the name of the story, and Hortensius asks : "How is that, a Romance in the 18th century?" Euph. "Yes, a Romance in reality and not a Novel. — A story like those of the middle ages, composed of Chivalry, Love, and Religion." They then proceed to discuss the book, Euphanasia remarking : "This work is distinguished in my

---

[1] Vol. I., page 102. (First edition.)      [2] See the *Advertisement.*
[3] Vol. II., page 31.

list, among Novels uncommon and Original." Sophronia erroneously gives *Longsword's* date of publication as 1766 instead of 1762.

Although Horace Walpole did so much for Romanticism, his own literary taste was not Romantic — in fact it was not good. His intense admiration for Gray's *Odes* may be largely accounted for by his personal attachment to their author, and by the fact that the *Odes* was the first publication from his own press at Strawberry Hill. Gray's later and more purely Romantic work was disliked and not appreciated by Walpole. In a letter to George Montagu, March 12, 1768, he said : "Gray has added to his poems three ancient odes from Norway and Wales. The subjects of the two first are grand and picturesque, and there is *his* genuine vein in them ; but they are not interesting, and do not, like his other poems, touch any passion. . . . Who can care through what horrors a Runic savage arrived at all the joys and glories they (*sic*) could conceive, the supreme felicity of boozing ale out of the skull of an enemy in Odin's hall?" Walpole also took little interest in Paul Henri Mallet's epoch-making *Histoire de Dannemarck.* In a letter to Montagu, February 19, 1765, he said : "I cannot say he has the art of making a very tiresome subject agreeable. There are six volumes and I am stuck fast in the fourth." Nor was Walpole much impressed by Ossian. At first he seemed to think the poems genuine, but he very soon changed his mind, and had no language strong enough to express his contempt for Macpherson and his writings — the one subject on which Johnson and Walpole agreed. He said : "It tires me to death to read how many ways a warrior is like the moon, or the sun, or a rock, or a lion, or the ocean." Again, Walpole constantly made fun of T. Warton's *History of English Poetry.* Writing to Mason, March 9, 1781, he said : "Mr. Warton thinks Prior spoiled his original in his imitation of 'Henry and Emma.' Mercy on us ! what shall we come to in these halcyon days?"

Walpole was at heart very much of an Augustan; his Romanticism was mainly a taste for novelties. To the last his favorite poet was apparently Pope. His letters contain many references to Thomson, of whom he spoke with the utmost contempt; and the significance of Thomson's Spenserian and nature poetry Walpole never seemed to feel. Of course, this contemptuous attitude was partly owing to the regular position which gentlemen took toward professional men of letters; of most contemporary authors he spoke with ridicule and disgust, crying out in 1746, "Pope and poetry are dead!" Nor did he spare Spenser and Shakspere. March 9, 1765, he wrote to Cole, "I am almost afraid I must go and read Spenser, and wade through his allegories, and drawling stanzas." He said of *A Midsummer Night's Dream*, that it was "forty times more nonsensical than the worst translation of any Italian opera-books."

All this, of course, furnishes still more evidence to one of the main propositions I have endeavored to establish — the unconsciousness of the English Romantic movement. Some of the men who did the most for Romanticism were really opposed to it in spirit.

Along with the revival of Gothicism in literature and art, came the revival of the love and study of Chivalry — indeed they were both parts of the same movement. Thomas Warton, in his *Observations on the Faery Queen* (1754), made a strong plea for the study of chivalry. He said that if the reader wished to understand Spenser, he must go back in imagination to the age in which Spenser lived. " For want of this caution, too many readers view the Knights and damsels, the tournaments and enchantments, of Spenser, with modern eyes; never considering that the encounters of chivalry subsisted in our author's age; that romances were then most eagerly read and studied; and that consequently Spenser, from the fashion of the times, was induced to undertake a recital of chivalrous achievements, and to become, in short, a *romantic* poet." [1] He closed his *Observations* with a defense of chivalry and a plea for more study of mediæval romances and mediæval life.

In 1762 appeared a very important work, *Letters on Chivalry and Romance*, by Bishop Richard Hurd (1720–1808). These letters were meant to be supplementary to III. and IV. of his *Moral and Political Dialogues*, published some years before. These two dialogues were headed *On the Age of Queen Elizabeth*, in which Mr. Digby, Dr. Arbuthnot and Addison were the speakers. Hurd took a bold position in the *Dialogues*, but he went still further in the *Letters*. He discussed the origin of chivalry, compared Heroic and Gothic manners, and declared the latter more poetical ; he showed their effect on Spenser and Milton, criticised the *Fairy Queen* and Tasso's epic, and finally traced the decline of Gothic poetry.

Hurd shows on every page the influence of the Warton brothers, but he took a much bolder and more confident position than either of them had dared to assume. Between 1756 and 1762 Romanticism had made rapid progress. Hurd's purpose was to vindicate Gothic manners and to show that they were superior to the Heroic as subjects for poetry. In his first *Letter* he said, " May there not be something in the Gothic Romance peculiarly suited to the views of a genius, and to the ends of poetry? And may not the philosophic moderns have gone too far in their perpetual ridicule and contempt of it? "

The word " Romantic " like the word " Gothic " was appreciating in value by being restored to something resembling its proper use. In *Letter III.* Hurd says, "*feudal* service soon introduced what may be truly called *romantic*, the *going in quest of adventures.*" In *Letter VI.* Hurd spoke of Gothicism in a way that must have dumbfounded many of his contemporaries. He said, " So far as the heroic and Gothic manners are the same, the pictures of each, if well taken, must be equally entertaining. But I go further, and maintain that the circumstances, in which they differ, are clearly to the advantage of the Gothic designers." He adds that if Homer had seen feudal manners, he would certainly have preferred them. "And the grounds of this preference would, I suppose, have been, *the improved gallantry of the Gothic Knights;* and the *superior solemnity of their superstitions."* [1]

Not satisfied with this, Hurd proceeded to do something that to the Augustan would have seemed blasphemous; he called the Grecian manners barbarous, saying that Gothicism furnished the poet "with finer scenes and subjects . . . than the simple and uncontrolled barbarity of the Grecian. . . . For the more solemn fancies of witchcraft and incantation, the Gothic (popular tales) are above measure striking and terrible."

The conclusion of *Letter VI.* is worth quoting. It shows how swiftly Romanticism was advancing. "We are upon enchanted ground, my friend; and you are to think yourself well used, that I detain you no longer in this fearful circle. The glympse, you have had of it, will help your imagination to conceive the rest. And without more words you will readily apprehend that the fancies of our modern bards are not only more gallant, but, on a change of the scene, more sublime, more terrible, more alarming, than those of the classic fables. In a word, you will find that the *manners* they paint, and the *superstitions* they adopt, are the more poetical for being *Gothic."*

Hurd claimed Spenser and Milton as witnesses on his side of the case of Gothicism *versus* Classicism, saying that Milton took the Classic model instead of the Gothic only after "long hesitation; his favorite subject was Arthur and his Knights of the Round Table." It is always an interesting occupation for the imagination to speculate on the style and character of the great Romantic poem which Milton had in mind, but which he finally abandoned. He might have created the greatest piece of Romantic literature in the English language.

[1] Italics always his own.

Hurd's discussion of the "Follow Nature" maxim, given in *Letter X.*, is suggestive. "But the source of bad criticism, as universally of bad philosophy, is the abuse of terms. A poet, they say, must follow *nature;* and by nature we are to suppose can only be meant the known and experienced course of affairs in this world. Whereas the poet has a world of his own, where experience has less to do, than consistent imagination. He has, besides, a supernatural world to range in. He has Gods, and Fairies, and Witches, at his command. . . . In the poet's world, all is marvellous and extraordinary; yet not *unnatural* in one sense, as it agrees to the conceptions that are readily entertained of these magical and wonder-working natures. This trite maxim of *following nature* is further mistaken, in applying it indiscriminately to all sorts of poetry." He then proceeds to compare the poetry of men and manners with the poetry that is "sublime and creative."

In this eminently sane discussion of two schools of poetry, Hurd was following directly in the path marked out by Joseph Warton in his *Essay on Pope* (1756). The peculiarly interesting thing about Hurd's tone is its contrast to the tone of criticism to-day. Hurd freely acknowledged the claim of the "follow nature" poetry; he simply wished to get a hearing for imaginative and Romantic poetry — in short, to persuade the public that such work might truthfully claim to be legitimate poetry. He succeeded so well that to-day the whole attitude of criticism is exactly reversed. Every one acknowledges imaginative and Romantic poetry, and stray critics like Mr. Courthope have to work harder than Hurd labored for his cause to persuade their generation that the poetry of men and manners is poetry at all.

Hurd was not particularly hopeful about the future of Romanticism. He had no conception of the far-reaching effect of his own work. His last *Letter* discussed the decline of Gothic poetry, and the revolution brought about during the Augustan age. He sadly remarked, "What we have gotten by this revolution, you will say, is a great deal of good sense.

What we have lost, is a world of fine fabling." He did not perceive with what gigantic strides the counter-revolution was about to move.

We must regard Hurd as a strong influence. (1) He was a follower of the Warton school of criticism, and spoke much more boldly and decisively than Warton for Romantic tastes.

(2) Besides helping in the general movement, he joined the Wartons in dethroning Pope by exalting the imaginative poets.

(3) He came just at the time to accelerate the speed of the Romantic movement. Hurd's learning and authoritative position counted for much; and the emphasis with which he spoke is remarkable, coming so early as 1762. The critical judgments on poetry made by Matthew Arnold are really a simple re-statement of what Joseph Warton and Hurd laid down a hundred years before.

From this time everything with a Gothic flavor rose rapidly in public esteem. The love of chivalry and the revival of Gothic architecture on the one hand, and the tremendous impetus which Percy gave to ballad literature on the other, formed two streams that flowed with increasing size and speed until they finally united in Walter Scott.

# CHAPTER VII.

## REVIVAL OF THE PAST — BALLAD LITERATURE AND PERCY.

It was natural enough that the old English ballads should not have been appreciated in the Augustan age. There can hardly be a greater contrast in style and sentiment than that between the freshness, spontaneity and wild music of the old songs of love and war, and the polished, artificial, monotonous strains of the Queen Anne didactic and satirical poetry. We shall find a few exceptions to the general taste; but the common attitude toward ballads was one of contempt or idle curiosity. Self-satisfied Augustan eyes looked upon them as barbarous — good enough, indeed, for the childhood of English literature, but not worth the serious attention of men who had learned the true art of poetry from Waller. With the exception of Garlands, no real collection of ballads appeared in the century till the year 1723. For years ballads had been neglected and scattered about the country in loose sheets, many of them serving for mural decorations, or stopping holes to expel the winter's flaw. In the seventeenth century, antiquarian scholars like Selden and Pepys began to make collections of this fugitive literature, regarding them of course in the light of curiosities, rather than as having any intrinsic literary value.

Among the Augustans, in spite of the general feeling, there was an occasional good word spoken for the old English ballads. In two numbers of the *Spectator*, May 21 and May 25, 1711, Addison wrote his critique of the ballad of *Chevy-Chase*.[1] The tone of Addison's criticism is somewhat suggestive;

---

[1] *Spectator*, Nos. 70 and 74.

he evidently appreciated the ballad, and at the same time was timid in avowing his taste, for he constantly quoted Vergil. He said that travelling had stimulated him to ballad-collecting, and then in deference to the "greatest modern critics," who contended that "an heroic poem should be founded upon some important precept of morality," he labored to prove that this requirement was satisfied in *Chevy-Chase.*

Addison also thought it necessary to apologize for the simplicity of the ballad. "I must only caution the reader not to let the simplicity of the style, which one may well pardon in so old a poet, prejudice him against the greatness of the thought."[1] He also remarked, "I shall . . . show that the sentiments in that ballad are extremely natural and poetical, and full of the majestic simplicity which we admire in the greatest of the ancient poets."[2] In conclusion, he spoke of the newness of the subject for his treatment and of the necessity for supporting his opinion by the authority of Vergil. "I shall only beg pardon for such a profusion of Latin quotations; which I should not have made use of, but that I feared my own judgment would have looked too singular on such a subject, had not I supported it by the practice and authority of Virgil."[3] This comparison of *Chevy-Chase* with Vergil is akin to Prior's attempt to serve two masters — Horace and Spenser. We find a secret love of the old English poetry, but public opinion demanded that everything should be tried by Classic models.

In the *Spectator* for June 7, 1711,[4] Addison spoke appreciatively of the ballad of *Two Children in the Wood*, saying it gave him "most exquisite pleasure." He also went a little further in the defense of ballads in general, saying that Lord Dorset and the poet Dryden had collections of ballads, and were fond of reading them, and that he knew that "several of the most refined writers of our present age" were "of the same humour."

[1] No. 70.    [2] No. 74.    [3] No. 74.    [4] No. 85.

Addison's ballad reviews, of course, attracted some attention, and in a small way contributed to the ballad revival;[1] but they produced no revolution in the public taste, nor did Addison ever intend that they should.[2]

Another Augustan writer did something for the ballad revival — Nicholas Rowe, the dramatist (1673–1718). In 1714 appeared *The Tragedy of Jane Shore. Written in Imitation of Shakespear's Style.* It is the prologue that is especially significant. He came out rather boldly for old English : —

> "Tonight, if you have brought your good old Taste,
> We'll treat you with a downright English feast.
> A Tale, which told long since in homely wise,
> Have never fail'd of melting gentle Eyes.
> Let no nice Sir despise our hapless Dame,
> Because recording ballads chaunt her name ;
> Those venerable ancient song-enditers
> Soar'd many a pitch above our modern writers ;
> They caterwaul'd in no romantick ditty,
> Sighing for Phillis's, or Chloe's pity."

This use of the word *romantick* is striking. The old ballads are just what we should call Romantic, but Rowe's use of the word shows how different and degraded a meaning it had among the Augustans. This Prologue must have required considerable courage on Rowe's part, as its tone was so exactly contrary to public taste.

As is well known, the poet Prior "versified" the ballad of the *Not-Browne Mayde* into the heroic couplet, under the title of *Henry and Emma* (1718). Prior undoubtedly thought that he had transformed the old ballad into real poetry, and the age thought so too. Still, his poem called attention to this fine piece of old literature, and in that way perhaps rendered some

---

[1] They certainly had some influence on the editor of the *Collection of Old Ballads* (1723).

[2] Dr. Johnson ridiculed all these ballad-praises in the *Rambler*, No. 177.

service to the movement.  He published the ballad itself along with his own version.[1]

In a chronological list of the collections of ballads and songs published between 1700 and 1765, the first work to deserve notice would be *A Choise Collection of Comic and Serious Scots Poems, both Ancient and Modern.  By Several Hands.  Printed by James Watson.*  This was published at Edinburgh in three volumes, the first part appearing in 1706, the second in 1709, the third in 1711.  The compiler of these songs is not known, but his name is generally supposed to have been John Spottis-wood.  The Preface was written by the publisher.  He called attention to the common fashion in other European countries of publishing miscellanies, and said he hoped this would justify his present enterprise.  "'Tis hoped, that this being the first of its nature which has been published in our own native Scots dialect, the candid reader may be the more easily induced, through the consideration thereof, to give some charitable grains of allowance, if the performance come not up to such a point of exactness as may please an over nice palate."

Watson's object was evidently not so much to revive old ballads as to make a song-miscellany.  But his collection was the fore-runner of a large number that followed, and he is chiefly significant as the main inspiration of the important work of Allan Ramsay.  Watson was a genuine pioneer, and for that reason holds a position of considerable importance in this branch of the Romantic movement.  Minto says that his book was the great seminal work of all the Scotch poetry of the century.[2]  His fresh, unaffected songs must have come like a cooling breeze over the arid wastes of contemporary verse.

In 1719 Ramsay published a collection of *Scots Songs.*  This is not of much importance, as it was so completely eclipsed

[1] In this connection, *Parnell's Fairy Tale in the Ancient English Style*, already spoken of in Chapter II., may be evidenced as another stray piece of literature showing a fondness for old English.

[2] *Ward's English Poets*, Vol. III., page 159.

by his later work. But it enjoyed some popularity, and ran through two editions.

In 1719–20,[1] at London, Thomas D'Urfey edited in six volumes, *Wit and Mirth; or Pills to Purge Melancholy; Being a Collection of the Best Merry Ballads and Songs Old and New. Fitted to all Humours, having each their proper Tune for either Voice, or Instrument; Most of the Songs being new Set.* Many of these songs were accompanied by the musical score; and the principal object of the collection was, of course, not to revive old English literature, but to make a popular singing-book. D'Urfey has, therefore, but little significance in the Romantic movement. His Dedication is curious enough to be worth quoting. "I have (with a great deal of trouble and pains) made some part of this collection, and render'd ye many of the old pieces which were thought well of in former days, . . . and I must presume to say, scarce any other man could have perform'd the like, my double genius for poetry and musick giving me still that ability which others perhaps might want." He then says he has performed his "own things" before King Charles II., King James, King William, Queen Mary, Queen Anne, and Prince George. D'Urfey's dedication is unmodest, and his songs are immodest. They are unspeakably loose and coarse, although intended for singing by young men and maidens. It is not strange that Ramsay thought his own collections clean, when the public tolerated such abominable stuff as D'Urfey raked together.

We come now to something quite different — a publication that has an important place in the history of the ballad revival. This was an anonymous work in three volumes, the full title being as follows : *A Collection of Old Ballads, Corrected from the best and most ancient Copies Extant. With Introductions Historical, Critical or Humorous. Illustrated with Copper Plates.* These important volumes were published in London, the first and second in 1723, and the third in 1725.[2] The

---

[1] Other editions came out earlier.

[2] The dates are very often given incorrectly. I took them directly from the title-pages of the original editions.

name of the editor has never been positively known, but he is supposed to have been Ambrose Philips, who wrote the Spenserian pastorals. The Prefaces to these volumes are significant. Like Addison, the Editor felt forced to appeal to the authority of the classics. In the preface to the first volume he said, " As the greatest part of this book is not my own, and several things in it written ages ago, I may, I hope, without either vanity or offence enter upon the praises of Ballads, and shew their antiquity." He remarks that " old Homer . . . was nothing more than a blind Ballad-singer. Pindar, Anacreon, Horace, Cowley, Suckling are Ballad-makers."

The Editor increased the usefulness of his volume by prefix-ing to many of the ballads historical and critical introductions. This research work went a long way toward disseminating knowledge about old English literature; and the strongest proof that this collection aroused general interest was its immediate and wide-spread popularity. Success encouraged the Editor to take a somewhat bolder tone. In the second edition of the first volume he said, " The encouragement which my design has met, especially from people of the best taste, has induced me to make a Second Collection, in which are contained a considerable number of Ballads more ancient and upon far older subjects than the generality of these; and from the pains I have taken not only with the introduction, but also to recover the best and oldest copies extant, I dare promise myself they will prove a grateful entertainment to the curious reader."

Among the ballads in the first volume was *Chevy-Chase*, of which the Editor remarked, " I shall not here point out the particular beauties of this song, with which even [1] Mr. Addison was so charm'd, that in a very accurate criticism upon it . . . he proves, that every line is written with a true spirit of poetry." This shows that Addison's criticism had had some effect.

---

[1] This "even" is suggestive.

In the preface to the second volume, published the same year (1723), the Editor congratulates himself on the popularity of his undertaking, saying "though we printed a large edition for such a trifle, and in less than two months time put it to the press again, yet could we not get our second edition out before it was really wanted."

It is interesting to observe that this Editor in 1723 thought it necessary to do just what Percy did in 1765 — he floated the old ballads by adding a number of modern popular songs. He also, again like Percy, adopted the apologetic tone. "There are many who perhaps will think it ridiculous enough to enter seriously into a dissertation upon ballads; and therefore I shall say as little as possibly I can." His defense was that although contemporary taste did condemn the ballads, they were not considered childish by the age in which they were written, but that their authors were able and prominent men. He concluded his preface by saying that he had material enough for another volume, but did not intend to let the world know whether or not he would publish it until the world had let him know whether or not they would encourage him. In two years (1725) he published the third volume, and said that it had been delayed by "divers accidents." In Vol. II. he had printed genuine old pieces like *Leir and his Three Daughters*, *King Arthur*, *Robin Hood*, and others; but in the third volume he weakened. He gave as his reason for omitting many old ballads, that they were "written in so old or obsolete a stile that few or none of my readers wou'd have understood 'em." Possibly the world had not encouraged him so much as he hoped; his tone is that of a man whose enthusiasm had been wet-blanketed by adverse criticism. Matters were different in 1765. The character and taste of the audience had changed.

Many filthy and immoral songs appeared in this early ballad collection. The attitude toward old ballads, as toward Spenser, seems hardly to have been one of sincere admiration. In many minds old English ballads were necessarily associated with coarseness, and when imitations of them were written people thought an alloy of smut was necessary, just as was the case with the imitations of Spenser.

Notwithstanding these defects, this collection of 1723–25 has deep significance. Its purpose was totally different from that of the ordinary song-miscellanies; it was an attempt at a genuine revival of old ballad literature, and points directly to Percy. Its great popularity is also note-worthy, even if it was a sudden blaze rather than a steady fire.

In 1724, Allan Ramsay (1686–1758) published two mis-cellanies of considerable importance, the *Tea-Table Miscellany* and the *Evergreen.* These works are usually classed together, as if they were entirely similar; in reality there is between them an important difference, as will presently appear. Ramsay brought out his miscellanies apparently without any knowledge of the *Collection of Old Ballads,* published the year before; for he must have begun collecting materials some time before that work appeared. Ramsay's inspiration goes back to James Watson. The dedication of the first volume of the *Tea-Table* is dated January 1, 1724. When the second volume appeared is not certainly known. It is usually ascribed to the same year, 1724, but there is no real evidence to support this date, as no copy of the first edition of the second volume is known to be extant. It seems better to ascribe it to the year 1725 or 1726, for Ramsay was also busy in 1724 with the *Evergreen,* and good evidence for the later date is furnished by the ballad of *William and Margaret,* a full discussion of which will be given later.[1] The third volume of the *Tea-Table* appeared in 1727, and the fourth volume with the tenth edition of the whole work in 1740. The *Tea-Table* was not exactly an attempt to revive old ballads, although it was a strong influence in the movement; it was really a song collection. Ramsay's object in this work was to amuse rather than to instruct the age. He included a number of modern songs, like *'Twas when the seas*

---

[1] See appendix.

*were roaring*, and other pieces. The tone of his preface shows that he had nothing revolutionary in mind. But although Ramsay's chief object was amusement, he brought to public attention some remarkable ballads, of which two may be mentioned — Hamilton's *Braes o' Yarrow* and *William and Margaret*, usually erroneously ascribed to David Mallet. The former was one of the most strictly Romantic productions of any author in the first half of the eighteenth century ; and the latter attracted wide-spread attention, not only on account of its merit, but because of Mallet's claim to its authorship. Ramsay included a number of his own pieces, his *Farewel to Lochaber* being one of the few serious songs he ever wrote, as well as one of the best. In the fourth volume appeared the old ballad of *Sweet William's Ghost*, and curiously enough, a coarse parody of *William and Margaret*, called *Watty and Madge*. The *Tea-Table* was enormously popular, and ran through a great number of editions ; it was steadily published till 1765.

The *Evergreen*, which appeared in two volumes, the dedication being dated October 15, 1724, is an altogether different work. The full title reads, *The Evergreen. Being a Collection of Scots Poems, Wrote by the Ingenious before 1600*. This was an attempt to awaken interest in old English poetry, and Ramsay's inspiration in this was not Watson, but the examples of the editors of Shakspere. The Dedication is written somewhat defiantly. "The Spirit of Freedom that shines throw both the serious and comick Performances of our old Poets, appears of a Piece with that Love of Liberty that our antient Heroes contended for." In the Preface, he remarked, "I have observed that Readers of the best and most exquisite Discernment frequently complain of our *modern Writings*, as filled with affected Delicacies and studied Refinements, which they would gladly exchange for that natural Strength of Thought and Simplicity of Stile our Forefathers practised : To such, I hope the following *Collection of Poems* will not be displeasing." His patriotism

and love of nature both appear in the following passage :
" When these good old *Bards* wrote, we had not yet made Use
of imported Trimmings upon our Cloaths, nor of foreign Em-
broidery in our Writings. Their *Poetry* is the Product of their
own Country, not pilfered and spoiled in the Transportation
from abroad : Their *Images* are native, and their *Landskips*
domestick ; copied from those Fields and Meadows we every
day behold." All this, of course, is bold talk for 1724 ; Ramsay is evidently comparing the rude, natural strength of old
English poetry with the insipid decorativeness of Augustan
style. He also gets in a hit at the couplet. " Besides, the
*Numbers*, in which these *Images* are conveyed, as they are not
now commonly practised, will appear new and amusing. The
different *Stanza* and varied *Cadence* will likewise much sooth
and engage the Ear, which in Poetry especially must be always
flattered."

Unfortunately the *Evergreen* was by no means such a success
as the *Tea-Table Miscellany*. A second edition did not appear
till 1761. Ramsay meant to issue a third and fourth volume,
but desisted, probably owing to the lack of encouragement that
the first two parts received.

Ramsay was not a scrupulous or conscientious editor. His
title-page announcement that the songs were " wrote before
1600 " is not strictly true. He palmed off as old ballads a
large number of new songs, and is thus, in a sense, the fore-
runner of Chatterton as well as of Percy. His own poem in
the *Evergreen*, called the *Vision*, he printed as " compylit in
Latin anno 1300 " and translated in 1524. Then, the ballad
*Hardyknute* was, of course, modern, though possibly Ramsay
himself did not know it. This ballad was an ingenious
imitation of the old English style, and deceived even so critical
a scholar as Gray, who said that he did " not at all believe "
the report that it was modern.[1] The poem was really written
by Lady Wardlaw of Pitrevie in Fife (1677–1726–7).

---

[1] Letter to Walpole, *Works* (ed. Gosse), Vol. III., page 45.

Ramsay made his compilation from the Bannatyne MSS., but omitted and added stanzas, modernized the versification and varied the spelling. He described the sources of his work in a poem which he wrote with the idea of prefixing it to the *Evergreen*, but perhaps his courage failed him, for the piece was not published till years afterwards. After naming over a list of authors, he says : —

> " Their Warkis I've publisht, neat, correct, and fair,
> Frae antique manuscriptis, with utmost cair."

But this is exactly what he did not do. At that time the Bannatyne MSS. were in the hands of William Carmichael, brother of the Earl of Hyndford; he lent them to Ramsay, who was neither sufficiently learned nor sufficiently scrupulous to edit them in any accurate or careful way. But it is not at all surprising that Ramsay's work was loose ; the surprising thing is that so early as 1724 such an attempt should have been made at all. The fact that one of Ramsay's miscellanies succeeded and the other failed seems to show that the age cared more for pretty songs than for any relics of antiquity. Due credit, however, should be given Ramsay for his own tastes. He is really one of the most remarkable figures in the early history of Romanticism. In both his creative and critical work, he threw his influence decidedly against the age. He brought before the public some thoroughly Romantic poetry, and stands as one of the pioneers among ballad collectors.

In 1724 appeared *The Hive. A Collection of the Most Celebrated Songs.* This was published anonymously, but was prefaced by *A Criticism on Song-writing. By Mr. Philips; in a letter to a lady.* If Philips really edited the *Collection of Old Ballads* (1723) he wrote his prefaces in an entirely different style from the way he talked here. In the *Hive* he says the French are the best song-writers, and that we cannot too highly praise the merits of the poet Waller. The *Hive* was popular, as by 1732 it had passed into a fourth edition. It is, however, simply one of the numerous group of song-miscellanies.

In 1725 William Thomson edited a large folio, containing the words and music of twenty-five songs. The full title was *Orpheus Caledonius, or a Collection of the Best Scotch Songs set to Musick by W. Thomson.* This book contained (without any acknowledgment) a number of the songs and poems that had appeared in the *Tea-Table,* and in later editions of his work Ramsay accordingly castigated Thomson. *Orpheus Caledonius* was but a slight contribution to the array of ballad collections and song-books, and has little significance in the movement.

In 1749 appeared *Warbling Muses,* a collection of lyrics edited by Benjamin Wakefield. On the title-page was printed the rather arrogant statement, " Being the first attempt of this Kind." The preface is very interesting, as showing the editor's attitude toward ancient and modern English literature. He says, " I selected a Multitude of Pieces from our most celebrated Poets, from *Shakespear* down to *Pope.* The Words of our famous modern Poets were sacred to me ; for which Reason I did not presume to alter a single Letter in them, except now and then a proper Name ; but I was far less scrupulous, with regard to the Compositions of such Poets of Eminence, part of whose Diction is grown obsolete ; I frequently modernizing many of their Expressions and harmonizing their Verse." The last sentence is especially good; we all know what was meant by the " harmonizing " process.

By the middle of the century the attempt to revive old ballad literature had all the appearance of being abortive. No steady public interest had been excited. But only ten years later we find signs of an interest in antiquity which very soon became a passion. In 1760 appeared one of the most scholarly bits of work that the whole century produced. This was a book by the afterwards famous Shaksperian editor, Edward Capell (1713–1781), called *Prolusions; or select Pieces of antient Poetry,—compil'd with great Care from their several Originals, and offer'd to the Publick as Specimens of the Integrity that should be found in the Editions of worthy Authors.* Capell therefore had a new aim — Accuracy — a thing in his time almost unknown, and in which he had few immediate imitators. In the dedication he said that his "honest intention" was to set editors an example of care and fidelity. The book was divided into three parts, the first being *The Notbrowne Mayde ; Master Sackvile's Induction ; and Overbury's Wife.* The second, *Edward the third, a Play thought to be writ by Shakespeare*, and the third division contained "Those excellent didactic Poems, intitl'd — *Nosce teipsum*, written by Sir John Davis ; with a Preface." Capell's preface to the *Prolusions*, dated July 20, 1759, explains the task of editing, and shows a respect for accuracy and fidelity that is almost modern ; he made some omissions and changes, but noted them all. He called his attempt in pub-lishing these old pieces a "novelty," which indeed it was. This work of Capell's gave to the public the fine ballad of the *Notbrowne Mayde* in its original, unmutilated and "unpolished" form. He simply ignored Prior's *Henry and Emma*, treating it with silent contempt. He gave the date of the ballad as early in the sixteenth century, saying that what "a poet of late days" (Prior) had said as to its age could not be true. In the revival of old literature, the *Prolusions* represents a distinct advance on previous work ; the editor was thoroughly in earnest, and assumed toward the poetry he revived no patronizing or apologetic tone. Capell has therefore some real significance in the Romantic movement.

Another indication of the growth of interest in antiquities, and a first fruit of Capell's work, appeared in 1764. No name is on the title-page of this volume, but its editor was John Bowle (1725–1788). The full title reads, *Miscellaneous Pieces of Antient English Poesie. viz The Troublesome Raigne of King John, Written by Shakespeare, Extant in no Edition of his Writ-ings. The Metamorphosis of Pygmalion's Image, and certain Satyres. By John Marston. The Scourge of Villanie. By the same. All printed before the year 1600.* This book, of course, does not strictly come under the head of ballad collections; but it evidenced a growth of the same interest, and belongs more properly to this part of the general subject than to any other. Bowle was influenced by Capell, and his book was another example of accuracy in scholarship. The text seems to have been printed with great care, and the original title-pages are reproduced. It is one of the best specimens of reprints that eighteenth century eyes ever beheld. Bowle was a man of great learning, who devoted himself to researches in obscure and untrodden paths; his specialty being Spanish literature.

We come now to the most famous ballad-book of the eighteenth century, Percy's *Reliques.* It was an epoch-making book, and is usually spoken of as one of the chief causes of the great re-awakening in English poetry. But the course of our studies in the ballad revival proves that Percy's book was fully as much a result as it was a cause of the Romantic movement. It is true that in the list of ballad collections that preceded Percy only two had much significance, the *Old Ballads* (1723-5) and Ramsay's *Evergreen* (1724). But the influence of these two was strong, and after 1755 evidences of renewed interest in antiquities — in poetry, chivalry, mythology — were showing themselves on every side. Percy's book came just at the critical time when the Romantic movement was beginning to be conscious of its own strength.

Thomas Percy (1729-1811) seems to have been interested in antiquarian researches from early youth. His tastes are shown by his publications. In 1761 he published *A Chinese Novel — Han Kiou Chooan*, in four volumes, translated by him from the Portuguese. In 1762 appeared *Miscellaneous Pieces Relating to the Chinese*, in two volumes. In 1763 he edited Surrey's poems, but with the exception of a few private copies, the whole impression was destroyed by fire. In 1763 appeared his *Five Pieces of Runic Poetry*. In 1764, *A New Translation of the Song of Solomon.* In 1765, the *Reliques.* In 1770, his translation of P. H. Mallet's book, *Northern Antiquities.* In 1771, his *Hermit of Warkworth.* In 1793, his *Essay on the Origin of the English Stage.* In 1782 he was made Bishop of Dromore in Ireland, and about 1806 he became blind.

Percy's correspondence with his friend Dr. Grainger, author of *Sugar-Cane,* also shows his interest in antiquities.[1] They discussed Macpherson's *Ossian* and similar subjects. Percy had evidently turned his inquisitive brain on Caribbean and American antiquities, for on July 25, 1762, Grainger writes : "I told you I could be of no service to you in promoting your intentional publications ; we have no old books of Knight-errantry in this island, and nobody can tell me anything of the Charibbean poetry; indeed, from what I have seen of these savages, I have no curiosity to know ought of their compositions. I have, however, desired a nephew of mine . . . who goes to-morrow to North America . . . to make all imaginable inquiry after the poetry of the North Americans. . . . If he has any success, you may depend upon my transmitting the effects of it to you."[2] This merely as a sample of Percy's passion for antiquarian bits of knowledge. His appetite grew by what it fed on.

For a number of years previous to 1765, Percy had been collecting materials for the *Reliques.* He bored his friends and acquaintances, and turned his keen glance in every direction. In justice to Shenstone, it should never be forgotten that it was he who first proposed the publication, and that he was to have been joint-editor. March 1, 1761, Shenstone wrote to his friend Graves, "You have perhaps heard me speak of Mr. Percy — he *was* in treaty with Mr. James Dodsley, for the publication of our best old ballads in three volumes. — He has a large folio MS. of ballads, which he shewed me,

---

[1] These letters are printed in Vols. VII. and VIII. of *Nichols's Literary Illustrations.*

[2] Nichols, Vol. VII., page 281.

and which, with his own natural and acquired talents, would qualify him for the purpose, as well as any man in England. I proposed the scheme for him *myself*, wishing to see an elegant *edition* and good collection of this kind, — I was also to have assisted him in selecting and rejecting; and in fixing upon the best readings — But my illness broke off our correspondence, the beginning of winter — and I know not what he has done since." [1]  Since 1742 Shenstone's taste had improved. His connection with Percy places him among the Romanticists.

The *Reliques* appeared in three volumes in February, 1765. The full title reads, *Reliques of Ancient English Poetry; Consisting of Old Heroic Ballads, Songs, and other Pieces of our Earlier Poets, (chiefly of the Lyric Kind). Together with some few of later Date.*
The chief sources of the *Reliques* were as follows:

1. The Folio MS.
2. Certain other MSS. collections.
3. Scotch ballads sent him by Sir David Dalrymple.
4. The ordinary printed broadsides.
5. Poems he extracted from the old printed collections. [2]

The MS. was a "scrubby, shabby, paper" book. Percy discovered it "lying dirty on the floor under a Bureau in ye Parlour" of Humphrey Pitt of Shiffnal. The servants had been accustomed to use it in kindling fires. Pitt gave it to Percy, who afterwards had it bound, a process in which the volume suffered considerably, often losing lines at the tops and bottoms of the pages. The date of the handwriting was probably about 1650.

Percy treated his materials in a way which nowadays would be considered scandalous, but which was common enough a hundred years ago. The influence of Capell and Bowle had not been strong enough to elevate very much the ideal of accuracy. It is extremely suggestive, however, to observe Percy's polishing, because it shows his own subservience to

---

[1] *Shenstone's Works*, Vol. III., page 363.
[2] This table is taken from the 1876 edition of the *Reliques*, Volume I., page lxxxi.

the public opinion which his book did so much to destroy. "As to the text, he looked on it as a young woman from the country with unkempt locks, whom he had to fit for fashionable society. . . . All fashionable requirements Percy supplied. He puffed out the 39 lines of the *Child of Ell* to 200; he pomatumed the *Heir of Lin* till it shone again; he stuffed bits of wool into *Sir Caroline, Sir Aldringar;* he powdered everything. The desired result was produced; his young woman was accepted by polite society, taken to the bosom of a countess, and rewarded her chaperon with a mitre."[1]

We observe, therefore, that in many respects Percy was not ahead of contemporary taste. This polishing and pruning process is proof sufficient; but the slight way in which he spoke of his book is also testimony to the point. Writing to Dr. Birch, February 2, 1765, he says, "I know not whether you will not be offended to find your name mentioned in the preface to such a strange collection of trash."[2] In later years, also, Percy looked on the *Reliques* as a youthful performance of no particular consequence; the fourth edition (1794) was edited by Percy's nephew, who said that the "original Editor had no desire to revive it."

But what is especially interesting in this connection is to notice in the original preface Percy's *apologetic* tone. He was evidently very timid in this undertaking, and afraid of popular ridicule. He bolstered himself up with the names of Shenstone and Dr. Johnson, the latter of whom he was very anxious to please. He said, "This manuscript was shown to several learned and ingenious friends, who thought the contents too curious to be consigned to oblivion, and importuned the possessor to select some of them, and give them to the press. As most of them are of great simplicity, and seem to have been merely written for the people, he was long in doubt whether, in the present state of improved literature, they could be

---

[1] Bishop Percy's Folio MS., Vol. I., page xvi.
[2] *Nichols*, Vol. VII., page 577.

deemed worthy of the attention of the public. At length the importunity of his friends prevailed, and he could refuse nothing to such judges as the author of *The Rambler* and the late Mr. Shenstone." Again he says, "In a polished age like the present, I am sensible that many of these reliques of antiquity will require great allowances to be made for them."

Percy also thought it necessary to do just what Ramsay and the Editor of *Old Ballads* had done; to float old ballads by adding modern lyrics. He says, "To atone for the rudeness of the more obsolete poems, each volume concludes with a few modern attempts in the same kind of writing; and to take off from the tediousness of the longer narratives, they are everywhere intermingled with little elegant pieces of the lyric kind."

Then, after naming a long list of eminent men to whose aid he was indebted, Percy added, "The names of so many men of learning and character the Editor hopes will serve as an amulet, to guard him from every unfavourable censure for having bestowed any attention on a parcel of Old Ballads." He then goes on to say that his "little work" has simply been the fruit of occasional leisure hours. Percy was evidently trying to cast anchors to windward. In studying the *Reliques*, this apologetic manner of the Editor should never be forgotten, for it constitutes further evidence toward the unconsciousness of the Romantic movement. Percy had no idea he had published an epoch-maker. The first edition appeared, as has been said, in 1765; the second in 1767. In the advertisement the editor speaks of the favorable reception given to his book. The second edition was very much like the first, except that the order of the pieces was changed, and the introductory essays considerably enlarged and improved. This advertisement is dated 1766, showing that a second edition was found to be necessary within a year. The third edition appeared in 1775. Further corrections were made, and Tyrwhitt's *Chaucer* was praised. The fourth edition did not appear till 1794, and was edited by the Bishop's nephew, Thomas Percy. A number of

corrections and improvements were made, and the text was
emended "by recurring to the old copies." The Editor took
occasion to reply to those who had doubted the existence of
any original MS., by giving a number of names as vouchers
and by describing the MS. in detail. But the folio was really
not so important to the *Reliques* as was, and still is, commonly
supposed. Percy said in his 1765 preface, that the "greater
part" of his material was extracted from the MS., but this was
not true; out of 176 pieces published in the *Reliques*, only 45
were taken from that source. Another example of eighteenth
century literary honesty.

In spite of the pains Percy had taken to forestall the criticism
of men like Johnson, he met with disappointment. Previously
to the publication of the *Reliques*, Percy and Johnson had
discussed the matter, and the Editor naturally thought that the
Doctor was on his side. But he should have remembered the
autocrat's fixed opinions on all literature of this stamp. In the
*Rambler* (No. 177) for November 26, 1751, Johnson had
ridiculed the taste for ballads and the black letter, and he was
not the man to change his mind. Although Johnson's limits
of appreciation were rather narrow, he had a sure nose for
anything Romantic. He was extremely suspicious of new
literary fashions. It was this instinct that led him to oppose
the Spenserians, to fight blank verse, to disparage Gray, and
to attack the taste for ballads; it led him also to make his
fierce onslaught on Macpherson. The Doctor gave the
*Reliques* no encouragement at all; and Warburton and even
Hurd had also recorded themselves against this kind of literary
work.

But if the critics looked askance at this new departure, the
popular reception was cordial and friendly enough to make all
amends. The *Reliques* reached the English heart, and stirred
up memories and aspirations that were full of promise for the
literature of the future. Dr. Grainger's letters to Percy show
the popularity of the work. In February, 1766, he wrote, "I

ᶦncerely congratulate you on the great success of your 'Ancient Poetry.' The book deserves all the applause which has been ᵍiven it." [1] A few months later he wrote, " I congratulate you again on the success of your 'Ancient Ballads'; though great, it is not more than they deserve." [2]

Percy's book makes the year 1765 one of the most important dates in the history of English Romanticism. The *Reliques* came just at the right time. Its effect on literature, though not felt so immediately as Ossian's, was far more healthful and far more lasting. It influenced the younger generation of readers with a force hard to overestimate ; and men like Wordsworth and Scott always gladly acknowledged what they owed to it. Scott's eagerness in its perusal and its effect on his taste are well known ; and Wordsworth's testimony as to its effect on the language is worth remembering. [3]

Besides the direct influence of the ballads, the prose matter Percy published with the *Reliques* had a wide influence. His *Essay on the Ancient Minstrels* inspired Beattie to write his Spenserian poem ; [4] and the other essays on antiquarian matters must have done much to stir up interest in the past. [5]

The best evidence as to the effect of Percy's book on English literature may be obtained by a glance at the ballad bibliography of the eighteenth century. [6] Before Percy, only two important collections had appeared ; in the remaining years they came as thick as tale. Ritson was a bitter opponent of Percy, and took a fiendish delight in exhibiting to the public the Bishop's loose methods of editing ; he stoutly denied the existence of the MS., and was silenced only by ocular proof.

---

[1] Nichols, Vol. VII., page 292.

[2] *Ibid.*, page 293.

[3] In *Poetry as a Study* (1815).

[4] *The Minstrel* (1771–1774).

[5] Besides the Essay already spoken of, the first edition of the *Reliques* contained essays on the "origin of the English stage," on the "metre of Pierce Plowman's Vision," and on the "ancient metrical romances"; and there were a great many interesting introductions to separate ballads.

[6] See list in Child's *Ballads* (1857), Vol. I., page xiii.

But Ritson owed much to the man he attacked ; and the excellence of his own work, and his important share in the ballad revival — where would it all have been without Percy ?

In 1823 an abridgment of the *Reliques* was published, called *Beauties of Ancient English Poetry.* The Preface may be partly quoted here, as showing how far the Romantic movement had progressed by that time and how much it owed to Percy. The Editor says, "Mr. Hume has observed that in the Fairy Queen of Spencer, the genius of the author is encumbered and disguised under the antiquated and fantastical costume of chivalry, which he has chosen to assume. We believe there are few readers of the poetry of the present day to whom this very objection does not constitute one essential interest and beauty of the work. . . . The feelings with which our ancient poetry was generally regarded at the beginning and close of the last century, were essentially different. In our Augustan age, as it has been termed, we see the mind of the country tending with determined force from that ancient literature, and in the present day we have seen its return upon these treasures of the past, with an almost passionate admiration." He then speaks of Goldsmith's ridicule of old poetry, saying, "No man will believe that Goldsmith, now living, would have so judged." All this is first-rate testimony to the profound and permanent influence of Percy's *Reliques*.

# CHAPTER VIII.

## REVIVAL OF THE PAST — NORTHERN MYTHOLOGY, WELSH POETRY, AND OSSIAN.

DURING the first half of the eighteenth century scarcely any interest seems to have been taken either in native superstitions or in Teutonic mythology. For poetic material the familiar Greek and Roman myths sufficed, and the superstitions of Scotland, Ireland and Wales shared the same neglect which had overtaken the old ballads. The first important poem in this branch of Romanticism was written late in the year 1749, but the public had no chance to see it until 1788. In 1749 Mr. John Home visited England to make some arrangements with Garrick about the stage presentation of the tragedy of *Douglas*. While Home was staying at the house of Mr. Barrow at Winchester, he met the poet Collins, and they evidently conversed on more or less Romantic themes, for after Home's return to Scotland, Collins sent him an ode he had just written, with the title, *An Ode on the Popular Superstitions of the Highlands of Scotland; considered as the subject of poetry; inscribed to Mr. Home, author of Douglas*. Strangely enough, neither Collins nor Home ever made any attempt to publish this Romantic poem. It was finally printed in 1788, by Dr. Alexander Carlyle, in the Transactions of the Royal Society of Edinburgh. Almost immediately afterward a rival edition also appeared ; and since that time this Ode has always ranked among Collins's most important work. The poem is in subject, treatment and style distinctly Romantic ; and it struck a new note in English verse. Mr. Lowell says, " The whole Romantic School, in its germ, no doubt, but yet unmistakably foreshadowed, lies already in the ' Ode on the Superstitions of the Highlands.' " [1] The

---

[1] *Literary Essays*, Vol. IV., page 3.

ninth stanza may be quoted, as an expression of the Romantic spirit in Collins : —

> " Unbounded is thy range ;  with varied skill
> Thy muse may, like those feathery tribes which spring
> From their rude rocks, extend her skirting wing
> Round the moist marge of each cold Hebrid isle,
> To that hoar pile, which still its ruin shows ;
> In whose small vaults a pigmy folk is found,
> Whose bones the delver with his spade upthrows,
> And culls them, wondering, from the hallowed ground !
> Or thither, where, beneath the showery west,
> The mighty kings of three fair realms are laid ;
> Once foes, perhaps, together now they rest,
> No slaves revere them, and no wars invade ;
> Yet frequent now, at midnight solemn hour,
> The rifted mounds their yawning cells unfold,
> And forth the monarchs stalk with sovereign power,
> In pageant robes, and wreathed with sheeny gold,
> And on their twilight tombs aërial councils hold."

It is an interesting fact that a poem of this nature, so different from the ordinary contemporary style, and so distinctly fore-shadowing later Romantic poetry, should have been suffered by the writer and by the one for whose sake it was written to lie so long in neglected manuscript.   In later years Collins might have published it, if his mind had not gone into an eclipse.   Perhaps Home thought it unsuitable for the taste of the age.   If it had been printed in 1750, it would doubtless have attracted attention.   It would certainly have pleased the Wartons and as certainly displeased Collins's firm friend, Dr. Johnson.

This Ode cannot be said to have done much for the Romantic movement, as it did not reach the public; but its composition is interesting as showing in what direction the mind of Collins was working, and that Romantic tastes were being generally, if secretly, cultivated.   Collins, like the Wartons, was an enthusiastic student of the old English authors.

The first book in Europe which aroused any general interest in Northern mythology and the literature of the Eddas, was written in the language which had done the most to preserve Classic style and form. This book was the *Introduction a l'Histoire de Dannemarck,* published in 1755. Its author was Paul Henri Mallet (1730–1807), a native of Geneva. In 1752 he had been made professor of Belles Lettres at Copenhagen, and had become deeply interested in Danish literature. His *Introduction* treated of the religion, laws, and customs of the ancient Danes, and was followed the next year (1756) by a second part, *Monuments de la mythologie et de la poesie des Celtes, et particulièrement des anciens Scandinaves.* In the same year his work was translated into Danish. In 1760 Mallet returned to Geneva, and by 1777 had completed his full *Histoire de Dannemarck.*

Throughout Europe the influence of Mallet's work was enormous, and for many years his book was the standard authority. Gray, always alert and watchful for any new literary event, was charmed. In his correspondence with Mason about *Caractacus,* in which Gray kept urging Mason to be as wild and picturesque as possible, he alluded to Mallet as follows (January 13, 1758): "I am pleased with the Gothic Elysium. Do you think I am ignorant about either that, or the *hell* before, or the *twilight.* I have been there, and have seen it all in Mallet's *Introduction to the History of Denmark* (it is in French), and many other places." [1] Gray also made other allusions to Mallet from time to time, which show that he was reading him carefully.

Mallet made a strong plea for the study of the customs and manners and mythology of the ancient Danes. He said, "The most affecting and most striking passages in the ancient northern poetry, were such as now seem to us the most whimsical, unintelligible, and overstrained. So different are our modes of thinking from theirs. We can admit of nothing

[1] *Gray's Works,* Vol. II., page 352.

but what is accurate and perspicuous. They only required bold and astonishing images which appear to us hyperbolical and gigantic." [1]   In the Introduction to Volume II., Mallet again returned to the charge.   " In fine, do we not discover in these religious opinions, that source of the marvellous with which our ancestors filled their Romances, a system of wonders unknown to the ancient Classics and but little investigated even to this day ; wherein we see Dwarfs and Giants, Fairies and Demons acting and directing all the machinery with the most regular conformity to certain characters which they always sustain." [2]

In the second volume Mallet gave a general description and historical sketch of the Eddas ; he translated a large portion of the Eddaic mythology, and also several Odes.   It was here that Gray got the hint for his *Descent of Odin.*   Mallet twice alludes to the poem,[3] and gives a translated extract.

Gray was not the only English man of letters who was stirred up by Mallet ; Percy seems to have become interested at about the same time, and he did English Romanticism an immense service by translating Mallet.   Percy's translation appeared in two volumes in 1770, with the title, *Northern Antiquities ; or a Description of the Manners, Customs, Religion and Laws of the Ancient Danes, and Other Northern Nations, including those of our own Saxon Ancestors, with a Translation of the Edda, or System of Runic Mythology, and other Pieces, From the Ancient Islandic Tongue.*   This translation included the first two volumes of the *Histoire de Dannemarck*, viz. — the *Introduction*, and the *Edda* with *Odes.*   The first volume consisted of a description of the arts, government and customs of the Danes, and a long discussion of their highly picturesque mythology. The translation of the Edda was given in the second volume ; the first part being the system of mythology, where stories of

---

1 English Translation called " Northern Antiquities," Vol. I., page 394.
2 Vol. II., page 9.
3 Vol. I., page 147, and Vol. II., page 220.

Odin, Frigga, Thor, Balder and the rest were told in dialogue; then followed some sketches of the *Elder Edda*, and translations of Odes.

To the English mind all this material was almost startlingly new. The wonderful richness and splendor of northern mythology and poetry were brought to popular knowledge just at the time when England was in a receptive attitude. All subsequent Norse study and all the revival of the Norse element in English literature may be traced back to Mallet's book.

Mallet, like all other men of the new school, assumed an apologetic attitude. He said, "But will not some object, To what good purpose can it serve to revive a heap of puerile fables, and opinions, which time hath so justly devoted to oblivion? Why take so much trouble to dispel the gloom which envelopes the infant state of nations? What have we to do with any but our own contemporaries? much less with barbarous manners, which have no sort of connection with our own, and which we shall happily never see revive again? This is the language we now often hear." [1] He then proceeds to refute such objections.

In discussing the new interest taken at this time in " Runic " poetry, it is an interesting fact that in the slender volume of poems by Thomas Warton, Senior, published in 1748, there are two Runic Odes. This strange contribution to Romanticism, coming years before Mallet, Percy and Gray drew public attention to Northern themes, is certainly noteworthy; and it is interesting to observe that the author of these two Runic odes was the father of the Warton brothers — affording additional evidence as to where they imbibed their Romantic tastes. Almost nothing is known to-day of this reverend gentleman ; but the remarkable ardor for Romanticism which his sons exhibited even from early youth may be partially explained by the fact that in their father's posthumous volume

[1] Vol. II., page 35.

we find both Spenserian and Runic poetry. Warton took
these two odes from Sir William Temple's essay *Of Heroic
Virtue.* Temple quotes with strong approval two Latin translations of a portion of the song of Regner Lodbrog, a Northern
king, who composed this poem "in the Runic language about
eight hundred years ago, after he was mortally stung by a
serpent, and before the venom seized upon his vitals." [1]
Temple remarked that in these verses there was a "vein truly
poetical." Warton's odes appear to be free translations from
this Latin, and as his poetry is so difficult of access, it may
be worth while to quote one of his Odes entire :—

> "At length appears the wish'd-for Night,
> When my glad Soul shall take her Flight ;
> Tremble my Limbs, my Eye-balls start,
> The Venom's busy at my Heart.
> Hark ! how the solemn Sisters call,
> And point aloft to *Odin's* Hall !
> I come, I come, prepare full Bowls,
> Fit Banquet for heroic Souls :
> What's Life ?— I scorn this idle Breath,
> I smile in the Embrace of Death !" [2]

Percy began his English translation of Mallet probably
about the same time that his *Reliques* appeared in print ; but
he had been reading Mallet earlier than that. In 1763
appeared a small anonymous volume, *Five Pieces of Runic
Poetry Translated from the Islandic Language.* On the
opposite side of the title-page a note was printed, "N. B.
This tract was drawn up for the press in the year 1761 ; but
the publication has been delayed by an accident." We see,
then, that Percy was working on Runic poetry in the same
year that Gray wrote his two Norse poems.

Percy was, of course, inspired by Mallet's book ; but it was
the success of the Ossianic fragments (1760) that induced him

---

[1] *Temple's Works* (1814), Vol. III., page 368.    [2] *Poems* (1748), page 159.

to publish. His preface is very interesting. After speaking of the roughness of the manners of the northern nations, he alludes to their "amazing fondness for poetry." A "few specimens of these are now offered to the public. It would be as vain to deny, as it is perhaps impolitic to mention, that this attempt is owing to the success of the Erse fragments. It is by no means for the interest of this little work, to have it brought into a comparison with those beautiful pieces, after which it must appear to the greatest disadvantage. And yet till the Translator of those poems thinks proper to produce his originals, it is impossible to say whether they do not owe their superiority, if not their whole existence, entirely to himself."

It is interesting to observe how the new interest in Norse mythology, the study of superstitions, the fragments of Gaelic verse, and various kinds of Romantic lore were all working together in the great literary movement. Anything wild and extravagant was now becoming as fashionable as it had previously been despised. Percy recommended his little volume by saying that "the poetry of the Scalds chiefly displays itself in images of terror."

The *Five Pieces* are prose translations of five Runic poems, with the originals added. Percy himself, however, had no first-hand knowledge of the language; the five poems which he gives had already appeared in Latin and Swedish versions. He obtained the assistance of a scholar, who compared these English versions with the originals, and who saw to it that the " Runic " was all right. Percy embellished his title-page with some Runic characters, both as an ornament and as a voucher that his poems were not forgeries. If *Ossian* had not already set the fashion of Romantic names, how strange must have sounded in eighteenth century ears titles like *The Dying Ode of Regner Lodbrog, The Ransome of Egill the Scald, The Funeral Song of Hacon!* The idea of putting them in *prose* must have been suggested to Percy by the success of Macpherson's experiment.    The Runic poems just hit the newly-aroused public sentiment.

A few quotations will show the style of the literature with which Percy fed the people. " Then the sword acquired spoils ; the whole ocean was one wound ; the earth grew red with reeking gore ; the sword grinned at the coats of mail ; the sword cleft the shields asunder." [1]

Then, as illustrative of the mythology : " We fought with swords. . . . From my early youth I learnt to dye my sword in crimson ; I never yet could find a man more valiant than myself. The gods now invite me to them. Death is not to be lamented. 'Tis with joy I cease. The goddesses of destiny are come to fetch me. Odin hath sent them from the habitation of the gods. I shall be joyfully received into the highest seat ; I shall quaff full goblets among the gods. The hours of my life are past away. I die laughing." [2]

We can easily imagine how Pope and Lady Mary would have criticised this style of poetry, and have " versified " it in correct couplets.

The Romantic movement was now making real progress. " Wild " poetry became all the rage, as we see by another sign of the times that appeared in 1764. This was a book by the Rev. Evan Evans (1731–1789), curate of Llanvair Talhaiam in Denbighshire. Evans was born at Cynhawdref, Cardiganshire, and studied at Oxford. From an early age he cultivated his love of poetry. He was a profound student of Welsh literature, and spent many hours transcribing Welsh MSS., and traveling about in Wales in search of material. He also composed Welsh poetry of his own. His important contribution to the Romantic movement is his work in 1764, *Some Specimens of the Poetry of the Antient Welsh Bards. Translated into English, with Explanatory Notes on the Historical Passages, and a short account of Men and Places mentioned by the Bards, in order to*

---

[1] *Dying Ode*, page 29.                    [2] Page 41.

*give the Curious some Idea of the Taste and Sentiments of our Ancestors, and their manner of Writing.*[1]

In this venture Evans claimed that he was not inspired by Ossian, but that he had had this book in mind for years. Possibly Gray's *Bard* may have suggested something to him, though he does not say so. He spoke with ardor of the wonderful style of Welsh poetry, and said "no nation in Europe possesses greater remains of antient and genuine pieces of this kind than the Welsh."

His description of his material is interesting. "The following poems . . . were taken from a manuscript of the learned Dr. Davies, author of the Dictionary, which he had transcribed from an antient vellum MS. which was wrote, partly in Edward the second and third's time, and partly in Henry the fifth's, containing the works of all the Bards from the Conquest to the death of Llewelyn, the last prince of the British line."

Evans makes no apology for Welsh poetry ; it is significant of the changing taste that he regards Extravagance as a drawing card. He says, "What was said of poetry in general, by one of the wits, that *it is but Prose run mad*, may very justly be applied to our Bards in particular ; for there are not such extravagant flights in any poetic compositions, except it be in the Eastern."

Evans's translations, like those of Macpherson and Percy, were in prose. He translated, in all, ten poems, and followed Percy's example in adding the originals. He also appended a treatise in Latin, *De Bardis Dissertatio.* One quotation from Evans's *Specimens* will suffice. "Llywelyn was our prince ere the furious contest happened, and the spoils were amassed with eagerness. The purple gore ran over the snow-white breasts of the warriors, and there was an universal havock and carnage after the shout. The parti-coloured waves flowed over the

---

[1] The copy I consulted was the original 1764 publication, in the Harvard library; it has many manuscript corrections in Evans's own hand, written November 9, 1772.

broken spear, and the warriors were silent. The briny wave came with force, and another met it mixed with blood, when we went to Porthaethwy on the steeds of the main over the great roaring of the floods. The spear raged with relentless fury, and the tide of blood rushed with force. Our attack was sudden and fierce. Death displayed itself in all its horrors; so that it was a doubt whether any of us should die of old age."[1]

Evans's *Specimens* has significance not only in its own connection with Ossianic poetry, but because it inspired Gray's poem, *The Triumphs of Owen*, published in 1768. Gray also composed some shorter Welsh pieces.

We come now to one of the most important literary events of the eighteenth century — the Ossianic poems of James Macpherson (1738–1796). Macpherson was born at Ruthven, Inverness, and after the year 1756 taught school there for some time. In 1759 he became acquainted with Home and Dr. Carlyle, and showed them some fragments of Erse poetry in his possession. Macpherson also told Dr. Blair that he was unwilling to publish these fragments, because they were so totally unlike the style of contemporary poetry that no one would pay any attention to them. But, emboldened by the encouragement of Blair, Home and Carlyle, he did publish, in 1760, *Fragments of Ancient Poetry Collected in the Highlands of Scotland, and translated from the Galic or Erse language.* Dr. Blair wrote a Preface for the work. (The *Fragments* is a small, thin volume, with no name on the title-page and nothing to indicate under whose sponsorship it appeared.) In this unassuming manner was published a book destined to arouse universal curiosity and excitement, and to exert a most powerful if not perpetual influence on English and Continental literature. In the preface we read, "The public may depend on the following fragments as genuine remains of ancient Scottish poetry. The date of their composition cannot be exactly ascer-

.ined. Tradition, in the country where they were written, refers them to an aera of the most remote antiquity; and this tradition is supported by the spirit and strain of the poems themselves; which abound with those ideas, and paint those manners, that belong to the most early state of society." Reference is then made to a supposed epic. "Though the poems now published appear as detached pieces in this collection, there is ground to believe that most of them were originally episodes of a greater work which related to the wars of Fingal. Concerning this hero innumerable traditions remain to this day, in the Highlands of Scotland. The story of Ossian, his son, is so generally known, that to describe one in whom the race of a great family ends, it has passed into a proverb, 'Ossian the last of the heroes.'" The passage just quoted is significant, as it affords either the excuse or the justification for the publication of the main poem in 1762. The preface also contained another bid for public interest. "It is believed, that, by a careful inquiry, many more remains of ancient genius, no less valuable than those now given to the world, might be found in the same country where these have been collected. In particular there is reason to hope that one work of considerable length and which deserves to be styled an heroick poem, might be recovered and translated, if encouragement were given to such an undertaking." This was a manifest feeling of the popular pulse. It was hoped that by printing just enough to inflame public curiosity, money would be subscribed sufficient to permit Macpherson to travel about the Highlands and collect more material. The scheme succeeded perfectly. Universal interest was aroused; and even Gray's delight is not surprising, for these early pieces do have intrinsic poetic merit, and the dose was not large enough to be nauseating. A quotation from Fragment VIII. is typical. "By the side of a rock on the hill, beneath the aged trees, old Ossian sat on the moss; the last of the race of Fingal. Sightless are his aged eyes; his beard is waving in the wind. Dull thro' the leafless trees he heard the voice of the north. Sorrow revived in his soul; he began and lamented the dead. . . . Fair with her locks of gold, her smooth neck, and her breasts of snow; fair as the spirits of the hill when at silent noon they glide along the heath; fair, as the rainbow of heaven; came Minvane the maid. Fingal! she softly saith, loose me my brother Gaul. Loose me the hope of my race, the terror of all but Fingal. Can I, replies the king, can I deny the lovely daughter of the hill? take thy brother, O Minvane, thou fairer than the snow of the north!"

This poetic prose was unlike anything that had yet been heard in England. Both scholars and general readers studied it eagerly; and Gray was fascinated. He immediately inquired of his friends on all sides, to furnish him further information and if possible to secure the originals. He could not make up his mind about the genuineness of the authorship. He corresponded with Macpherson, and said that the letters he received in return were "ill wrote, ill reasoned, unsatisfactory, calculated (one would imagine) to deceive one, and yet not cunning enough to do it cleverly. . . . In short, this man is the very Dæmon of poetry, or he has lighted on a treasure hid for ages." [1] But Gray was more inclined in this matter to faith than to skepticism, and though never positive and dogmatic, he always favored the theory of genuine authorship. Percy was also deeply interested, and asked Dr. Grainger for an opinion. Grainger replied, "Depend upon it, the 'Fragments' are not translated from the Erse; there is not one local or appropriated image in the whole. . . . The author, however, is a man of genius." [2] Percy was not satisfied, and wrote to Grainger again, but received substantially the same reply. Horace Walpole was evidently not deeply impressed with the poems. On receiving the first bits, he wrote to Dalrymple, February 3, 1760, "They are poetry, and resemble

---

[1] *Gray's Works*, Vol. III., page 51.
[2] *Nichols's Lit. Illus.*, Vol. VII., page 275.

that of the East; that is, they contain natural images and natural sentiment elevated, before rules were invented to make poetry difficult and dull." Walpole told Dalrymple that the poems would make an impression on Gray, and this explains how the latter received specimens so early. Walpole wrote again to Dalrymple, April 4, 1760, describing the effect the poetry had produced; he said that Gray, Mason, Lyttleton and one or two more were "in love with your Erse elegies; I cannot say in general they are so much admired." Walpole grew less and less pleased with the Ossianic poetry, and ended in complete skepticism and disgust, finally writing Mason September 17, 1776, "Oh! there is another of our authors, Macpherson! when one's pen can sink to him, it is time to seal one's letter." The above quotations illustrate the various opinions which the *Fragments* brought out. Enough interest was aroused to furnish Macpherson with sufficient funds to travel in search of that epic which in the preface to the *Fragments* had been so mysteriously alluded to.

The Epic seemed easy to find. The *Fragments* had been published in Edinburgh; the scene of the literary war was now boldly transferred to London. In 1762[1] a thick quarto was published: *Fingal, an Ancient Epic Poem, in Six Books: Together with several other Poems, composed by Ossian the Son of Fingal. Translated from the Galic Language, by James Macpherson.* With this volume appeared an Advertisement, a Preface, and a *Dissertation concerning the Antiquity, etc., of the Poems of Ossian the Son of Fingal,* all by Macpherson. In addition to the epic, this volume also contained sixteen short poems. Macpherson's preface is interesting. He defends himself against the charge of forgery, and also apologizes for the book. He feared the temper of the age would hardly stand the Ossianic style, or take any interest in the relics of

1 The date 1762 is on the title-page, and this is always given as the correct date. It must have appeared a little earlier, however, for Walpole writes, December 8, 1761, "Fingal is come out."

antiquity. He said, " I would not have dwelt so long upon
this subject, . . . were it not on account of the prejudices
of the present age against the ancient inhabitants of Britain."
He spoke of the interest aroused by the *Fragments*, and of
the " people of rank and taste " who had given him the funds
to search for *Fingal*.

Macpherson did not stop here. In 1763 appeared *Temora,
an Ancient Epic Poem, in Eight Books: Together with several
other Poems, composed by Ossian, the Son of Fingal. Translated
from the Galic Language, by James Macpherson.* There were five
"other poems," and a specimen of the original "Galic" of
*Temora*, together with a fresh Dissertation. He said of Ossian,
" His ideas, though remarkably proper for the times in which
he lived, are so contrary to the present advanced state of
society, that more than a common mediocrity of taste is
required, to relish his poems as they deserve." By this time
Macpherson was thoroughly stirred up by the attacks of the
critics, and his Dissertation is full of polemics. " I am
thoroughly convinced, that a few quaint lines of a Roman or
Greek epigrammatist, if dug out of the ruins of Herculaneum,
would meet with more cordial and universal applause than all
the most beautiful and natural rhapsodies of all the Celtic
bards and Scandinavian Scalders that ever existed."

It is important to remember that Macpherson himself was
no Romanticist. He never intended to establish a Romantic
school; in fact, his own taste was of the regulation eighteenth
century stamp. Some Irish fragments had been compared
with Ossian, and Macpherson ridiculed them on the ground
of their Romanticism. He said, "They are entirely writ in
that romantic taste, which prevailed two ages ago, — Giants,
enchanted castles, dwarfs, palfreys, witches and magicians
form the whole circle of the poet's invention. The celebrated
*Fion* could scarcely move from one hillock to another, without
encountering a giant, or being entangled in the circles of a
magician. Witches, or broomsticks, were continually hovering

around him, like crows ; and he had freed enchanted virgins
in every valley in Ireland.  In short, *Fion*, great as he was,
had but a bad sort of life of it."  He attacked Romanticism
again in a note to the poem *Cathloda*, but here he was trying
more to pacify his critics than to express his own views.
Speaking of the Highland bards he says, "They then launched
out into the wildest regions of fiction and romance.  I firmly
believe, there are more stories of giants, enchanted castles,
dwarfs, and palfreys, in the Highlands, than in any country
in Europe.[1]  These tales, it is certain, like other romantic
compositions, have many things in them unnatural, and consequently, disgustful to true taste, but, I know not how it happens,
they command attention more than any other fictions I ever
met with."  Macpherson had no idea that he was furthering
a genuine Romantic revolution.

In 1763 appeared Dr. Hugh Blair's ponderous essay, *A
Critical Dissertation on the Poems of Ossian, the Son of Fingal.*
This essay was bound in with *Fingal* and *Temora*, and continued
to appear in successive editions of these poems.  It is unspeakably dry, and is written in the minute style — criticising detail
after detail — so characteristic of eighteenth century literary
criticism.  He discussed at wearisome length the morality of
Ossian, and the essay is chiefly taken up with a comparison
of Ossian and Homer, a comparison that was as inevitable as
it was profitless.  There are, however, some points of interest
in this wilderness, especially where Blair tried to defend
Ossianic poetry.  He said Ossian's two great characteristics
were tenderness and sublimity.  "The events recorded are all
serious and grave ; the scenery throughout, wild and romantic.
The extended heath by the seashore ; the mountains shaded
with mist ; the torrent rushing through a solitary valley ; the
scattered oaks, and the tombs of warriors overgrown with moss ;
all produce a solemn attention in the mind, and prepare it for

---

[1] The tone of this is hardly consistent with his remarks on the Irish fragments,
which he said were spurious because so Romantic.

great and extraordinary events. We find not in Ossian an imagination that sports itself, and dresses out gay trifles to please the fancy. His poetry, more perhaps than that of any other writer, deserves to be styled, *The poetry of the heart."* Again : — "We meet with no affected ornaments ; no forced refinement ; no marks either in style or thought of a studied endeavor or to shine and sparkle. Ossian appears everywhere to be prompted by his feelings." In this way Blair helped along the Ossianic movement of sentimentalism, melancholy, and love of nature's solitudes ; what was called Wertherism in Germany might have been called Ossianism in England. It was along these lines that the influence of Ossian was most strongly felt on contemporary literature ; Ossian belongs largely to the subjective side of Romanticism, which culminated in England in the poet Byron.

Part of the Ossian excitement was due to Scotch patriotism — newly inflamed both by these publications and by the English adverse criticisms. Much of the opposition to Ossian was owing, of course, to English prejudice. The most cultivated men in Edinburgh were up in arms to defend their epic ; while the London critics, headed by the redoubtable Johnson — doubly armed by national feeling and literary classicism — continued to attack Ossian with argument and ridicule.

In the 1773 edition, Macpherson spoke of the warm welcome Ossian had received on the Continent ; he dwelt on its immense popularity in Europe, the successive versions that had appeared in various languages, and remarked that he now resigned the poems forever to their fate. He also spoke of the doubt that had originally perplexed him — whether to translate Ossian in prose or in verse — saying that he himself had preferred rime, but that he had been dissuaded from this by his friends. He also gives a specimen of his own Ossian couplets.

This point is certainly significant, as it shows Macpherson's own lack of judgment and inability to appreciate the signs of the times. Ossian in heroic couplets would almost certainly have fallen flat, or at best been extremely short-lived. And the tediousness of the tropes would have been centupled in the monotony of the rimes. Ossian certainly had a narrow escape. It was Macpherson's embossed and flowing rhetoric that did much to produce the extraordinary effect that followed his publications. Fetters both of thought and of language were everywhere being cast aside ; and it was largely owing to this popular weariness of effete formalism that Ossian was hailed with so intense eagerness. Its wildness, melancholy, sublimity — entire disregard of conventionality — these were the qualities that gave Ossian its enormous popularity. Ossian struck a note in perfect harmony with Rousseau's " Back to Nature " cry in France and with the *Sturm und Drang* in Germany ; in the latter country the poems were especially influential ; for the tide of sentimentalism was beginning to sweep everything before it. Werther's fondness for Ossian shows Goethe's appreciation of its significance ; and Chateaubriand was a pronounced admirer of Ossian — an important fact, because in Chateaubriand critics are usually agreed that French Romanticism had its primal impulse.

Ossian points as directly to Byron as the chivalry and ballad revivals point to Scott. These indicate the two great streams in the Romantic movement. In Byron's poetry — sincere or feigned — we see constantly manifest the Ossian feeling. What Byron himself thought of Ossian I have had a good opportunity to observe by perusing Byron's own manuscript notes in a copy of the Ossian poems.[1] The following notes I copied directly from Byron's hand-writing : " The portrait which Ossian has drawn of himself is indeed a masterpiece. He not only appears in the light of a distinguished warrior — generous as well as brave — and possessed of exquisite sensibility — but of an aged venerable bard — subjected to the

---

[1] It is the second volume of the 1806 edition of Ossian. The volume contains Byron's autograph and copious notes written in his own hand. This book is in the Harvard library.

most melancholy vicissitudes of fortune — weak and blind —
the sole survivor of his family — the last of the race of Fingal.
The character of Fingal — the poet's own father — is a highly
finished one.   There is certainly no hero in the Iliad — or
the Odyssey — who is at once so brave and amiable as this
renowned king of Morven.   It is well known that Hector —
whose character is of all the Homeric heroes the most complete
— greatly sullies the lustre of his glorious actions by the insult
over the fallen Patroclus.   On the other hand the conduct of
Fingal appears uniformly illustrious and great — without one
mean or inhuman action to tarnish the splendour of his fame —
He is equally the object of our admiration esteem and love."
Speaking of Ossian's skill in depicting female characters, he
writes, "How happily, for instance, has he characterized his
own mistress — afterwards his wife — by a single epithet ex-
pressive of that modesty — softness — and complacency —
which constitute the perfection of feminine excellence — 'the
mildly blushing Everallin.' . . .   I am of opinion that though
in sublimity of sentiment — in vivacity and strength of description — Ossian may claim a full equality of merit with Homer
himself — yet in the invention both of incidents and character
he is greatly inferior to the Grecian bard."

These quotations are interesting as showing how seriously
Byron took Ossian and how carefully and thoughtfully he read
him.  The influence of Ossian lasted long after the immediate
excitement caused by its novelty and professed antiquity had
passed away.

*1 Coleridge*

*2. Byron*

*3.*

## CHAPTER IX.

## THE ROMANTIC MOVEMENT EXEMPLIFIED IN GRAY.

A chronological study of Gray's poetry and of the imagination and love of nature displayed in his prose remains, is not only deeply interesting in itself, but is highly important to the history of Romanticism. In him, the greatest literary man of the time, we find the best example of the steady growth of the Romantic movement. But before proceeding to the discussion of this, a word on Gray's sterility is necessary. The view given by Matthew Arnold in his famous essay[1] is entirely without foundation in fact. The reason why Gray wrote so little was not because he was chilled by the public taste of the age; he would probably have written no more had he lived a hundred years before or since. He was not the man to be depressed by an unfavorable environment; for his mind was ever open to new influences, and he welcomed with the utmost eagerness all genuine signs of promise. His correspondence shows how closely and intelligently he followed the course of contemporary literature; he had something to say about every new important book. The causes of his lack of production are simple enough to those who start with no pre-conceived theory, and who prefer a commonplace explanation built on facts to a fanciful one built on phrases. Gray was a scholar, devoted to solitary research, and severely critical; this kind of temperament is not primarily creative, and does not toss off immortal poems every few weeks. The time that Mason spent in production, Gray spent in acquisition, and when he did produce, the critical fastidiousness of the scholar appeared in

[1] Ward's English Poets, Vol. III., p. 302.  Both Mr. Perry and Mr. Gosse seem to support Arnold's view, but I am unable to see anything in it.

every line. All his verses bear evidence of the most pains-taking labor and rigorous self-criticism. Again, during his whole life he was handicapped by wretched health, which, although never souring him, made his temperament melan-choly, and acted as a constant check on what creative activity he really possessed. And finally, he abhorred publicity and popularity. No one who reads his correspondence can doubt this fact. He hated to be dragged out from his scholarly seclusion, and evidently preferred complete obscurity to any noisy public reputation. This reserve was never affected; it was uniformly sincere, like everything else in Gray's character. His reticence was indeed extraordinary, keeping him not only from writing, but from publishing what he did write.[1] His own friends would have had no difficulty in explaining his scantiness of production. Horace Walpole, writing to George Montagu, Sept. 3, 1748, says: "I agree with you most abso-lutely in your opinion about Gray; he is the worst company in the world. From a melancholy turn, from living reclusely, and from a little too much dignity, he never converses easily; all his words are measured and chosen, and formed into sen-tences; his writings are admirable; he himself is not agree-able." Again, referring to Gray's slowness in composition, Walpole writes to Montagu, May 5, 1761. He is talking about Gray's proposed history of poetry, and he says: "If he rides Pegasus at his usual foot-pace, (he) will finish the first page two years hence." The adjective that perhaps best expresses Gray is *Fastidious*. He was as severe on the children of his own brain as he was on those of others; he never let them appear in public until he was sure everything was exactly as it should be. Even his greatest poem pleases more by its ex-quisite finish than by its depth of feeling. These three reasons, then, his scholarly temperament, his bad health, and his dignified reserve, account satisfactorily for his lack of

[1] He wrote, in English and Latin, more than 60 poems, but only 12 appeared in print during his lifetime; and his prose is all posthumous.

fertility. If we wish to know why so deep and strong a nature produced so little poetry, we must look at the man, and not at his contemporaries. So much for Gray's sterility.[1]

Although Gray's biographers and critics have very seldom spoken of it, the most interesting thing in a study of his poetry — and the thing, of course, that exclusively concerns us here — is his steady progress in the direction of Romanticism. Beginning as a classicist and disciple of Dryden, he ended in thorough-going Romanticism.[2] His early poems contain nothing Romantic; his *Elegy* has something of the Romantic mood, but shows many conventional touches; in the Pindaric Odes the Romantic feeling asserts itself boldly; and he ends in enthusiastic study of Norse and Celtic poetry and mythology. Such a steady growth in the mind of the greatest poet of the time shows not only what he learned from the age, but what he taught it. Gray is a much more important factor in the Romantic movement than seems to be commonly supposed. This will appear from a brief examination of his poetry.

While at Florence in the summer of 1740, he began to write an epic poem in Latin, *De Principiis Cogitandi.* Only two fragments were written,[3] but they made a piece of considerable length. This was an attempt to put in poetic form the philosophy of Locke. It shows how little he at that time understood his own future. The Gray of 1760 could no more have done a thing of this sort, than he could have written the *Essay on Man.* In these early years he was completely a Classicist. In 1748, when he was largely under Dryden's

1 After I had fully reached this conclusion, I read Mr. Tovey's recent book, *Gray and His Friends*. The *Introduction* to that book is the most judicious essay on Gray that I have ever seen in print, though Mr. Tovey does not discuss his connection with Romanticism. I was pleased to find that my view of Gray's sterility was very similar to Mr. Tovey's, who completely disposes of Arnold's theory.

2 He never despised Dryden, however, though he went far beyond him. Oct. 2, 1765, he wrote to Beattie, " Remember Dryden, and be blind to all his faults." *Gray's Works,* Vol. III., p. 221.

8 The second in 1742.

influence, he began a didactic poem in the heroic couplet, *On the Alliance of Education and Government*. It is significant that he never finished either of these poems. Mathias said: "When Mr. Nichols once asked Mr. Gray, why he never finished that incomparable Fragment on 'The Alliance between good Government and good Education, in order to produce the happiness of mankind,' he said, *he could not;* and then explained himself in words of this kind, or to this effect: 'I have been used to write chiefly lyrick poetry, in which, the poems being short, I have accustomed myself to polish every part of them with care; and as this has become a habit, I can scarcely write in any other manner; the labour of this in a *long* poem would hardly be tolerable.'"[1] Gray must have perceived early in this task that the game was not worth the candle.

In 1742 Gray wrote three Odes: *On the Spring*, *On a Distant Prospect of Eton College*, and *To Adversity*. These well-known pieces contain little intimation of Gray's later work. They have nothing of the spirit of Romanticism, and might have been written by any Augustan of sufficient talent. The moralizing is wholly conventional, and the abundance of personified abstractions was in the height of fashion. The poems thus far mentioned represent Gray's first period. He was a disciple of Dryden, and a great admirer of Pope, for writing to Walpole in 1746, he calls Pope "the finest writer, one of them, we ever had."[2]

Gray's second period is represented by the *Elegy*, which he began in 1742 and finished in June, 1750.[3] He was in no haste to print it; the manuscript circulated among his friends, and was first printed anonymously, with a preface by Horace

---

[1] *Mathias's Observations* (1815), page 52. This passage in itself goes a long way toward explaining Gray's sterility.

[2] *Gray's Works*, Vol. II., page 130.

[3] Gray's interesting letter to Walpole about the *Elegy*, June 12, 1750, may be found in his *Works*, Vol. II., page 209. He says: "You will, I hope, look upon it in the light of a thing with an end to it; a merit that most of my writings have wanted." He evidently felt the fragmentary nature of his previous work.

Walpole, February 16, 1751. How long Gray meant to keep the *Elegy* from the public is uncertain; circumstances compelled its publication. On February 10, 1751, the editor of the *Magazine of Magazines* requested permission to print it. This alarmed Gray; he flatly refused the editor's request, and wrote instantly to Walpole, asking him to get Dodsley to print it as soon as possible.[1]

The *Elegy* is not a Romantic poem; its moralizing is conventional, and pleased eighteenth century readers for that very reason. Scores of poems were written at that time in which the thought was neither above nor below that of the *Elegy*, and these poems have nearly all perished. What has kept Gray's contribution to the Church-yard school alive and popular through all changes in taste, is its absolute perfection of language. There are few poems in English literature that express the sentiment of the author with such felicity and beauty. This insures its immortality; and it is this fact that deservedly gives it the first place in Gray's literary productions.

But although the *Elegy* is not strictly Romantic, it is different from Gray's earlier work. It is Romantic in its *mood*, and stands as a transition between his period of Classicism and his more highly imaginative poetry. It was the culmination of the *Il Penseroso* school, and as I have shown, that school was in several ways intimately connected with the growth of the Romantic movement. There is one highly significant fact about the composition of the *Elegy*, which shows with perfect distinctness that its author was passing through a period of transition. One of its most famous stanzas Gray originally wrote as follows : —

> "Some Village Cato    with dauntless Breast
>     The little Tyrant of his Fields withstood ;
> Some mute inglorious Tully here may rest ;
>     Some Cæsar, guiltless of his Country's Blood."

[1] This letter is in *Gray's Works*, Vol. II., page 210. It contains minute instructions about the printing of the poem, and says it must be published anonymously.

The fact that Gray should originally have put down the Latin names, and afterwards inserted in their place the three names Hampden, Milton, Cromwell — taken from comparatively recent English history — is something certainly worth attention. It marks the transition from Classicism to Nationalism. In this stanza he shook off the shackles of pseudo-classicism; he made up his mind that English historical examples were equal in dignity to those taken from Latin literature. It was a long step forward, and although perhaps a small thing in itself, is an index to a profound change going on in Gray's mind.[1]

Gray's next work shows him well on the way toward Romanticism. In 1754 he wrote *The Progress of Poesy,* and in the same year began *The Bard,* which he finished in 1757. Both these Pindaric Odes were first printed in 1757, on Horace Walpole's press at Strawberry Hill — the first and the best things ever published there. These two odes, especially the latter, are the most imaginative poetry Gray ever produced, and were distinctly in advance of the age. They were above the popular conception of poetry, and their obscurity was increased by their allusiveness. The public did not take to them kindly ; many people regarded them as we see Browning and Wagner regarded to-day. Their obscurity was ridiculed, and they were freely parodied.[2] Gray was a little hurt by all this, but he had foreseen their probable reception. He had written to Walpole, " I don't know but I may send him (Dodsley) very soon . . . an ode to his own tooth, a high Pindaric upon stilts, which one must be a better scholar than he is to understand a line of, and the very best scholars will

---

[1] This point is fully and suggestively treated in the *Saturday Review* for June 19, 1875, in an article called *A Lesson from Gray's Elegy.*

[2] Dr. Johnson said they were " two compositions at which the readers of poetry were at first content to gaze in mute amazement." In 1783, Dr. Johnson was violently attacked for this by the Rev. R. Potter, an enthusiastic admirer of Gray. Potter said that Gray's *Bard,* with its " wild and romantic scenery," etc., was " the finest ode in the world."

understand but a little matter here and there." [1] Horace Walpole never forgave the age for its attitude toward Gray's odes. Again and again he refers to it in his correspondence, and it had much to do with his dislike for Dr. Johnson. [2] Walpole called the *Odes* "Shakspearian," "Pindaric," and "Sublime," and said they were "in the first rank of genius and poetry." But Walpole's opinions were largely influenced in this matter by personal pride, for his own taste was not at all reliable. He said Gray's *Eton Ode* was "far superior" to the *Elegy*. [3]

In the Pindaric *Odes*, Gray ceased to follow the age; he struck out ahead of it, and helped to mould its literary taste. From this time people began to regard him as a Romanticist, and to look for wild and extravagant productions from his pen. When the *Castle of Otranto* appeared in 1764, Gray was by many believed to be the author. The *Odes* became much more popular after Gray's death — a sign of growth in public taste. This made Dr. Johnson angry, and had much to do with his satirical treatment of the *Odes* in his wretched *Life of Gray*. He did not like to think that Gray had really taught the people anything, and so he declared that the admiration for Gray was all hypocrisy, just as many honest people to-day make fun of those who admire Wagner's music. Johnson said that in Gray's *Odes* "many were content to be shewn beauties which they could not see." Undoubtedly Gray and Wagner have hypocrites among their admirers; but the fact that each helped to set a fashion is significant of a change in taste.

We now enter upon the last period of Gray's literary production. In 1755 Mallet's *Introduction a l'Histoire de Dannemarck* appeared. This had a powerful effect on Gray, and aroused

---

1 *Works*, Vol. II., page 218.

2 For Walpole's remarks on Gray's *Odes*, see his letters to Horace Mann, August 4, 1757, and to Lyttleton, August 25, 1757. See especially his letter to Mason, January 27, 1781, on Johnson's *Life of Gray*. Walpole afterward spoke of Johnson as a "babbling old woman." and a "wight on stilts."

3 Letter to Lyttleton, August 25, 1757.

his interest in Northern mythology, which he studied with the utmost enthusiasm. In 1761, Gray wrote *The Fatal Sisters. From the Norse Tongue;* also *The Descent of Odin.* Evans's book on Welsh poetry, the *Specimens* (1764), stirred him up again, and he wrote *The Triumphs of Owen.* These three poems were published in 1768, in the edition of his writings revised by himself. All this work, of course, is strictly Romantic.[1] In 1760, when the Ossianic *Fragments* appeared, Gray was wonderfully aroused. His friends knew he would be excited, for Walpole, writing to Dalrymple, April 4, 1760, said, "You originally pointed him out as a likely person to be charmed with the old Irish poetry you sent me." On receiving some specimens, Gray immediately wrote to Walpole as follows: "I am so charmed with the two specimens of Erse poetry, that I cannot help giving you the trouble to inquire a little farther about them and should wish to see a few lines of the original, that I may form some slight idea of the language, the measures, and the rhythm."[2] He then proceeds to make further comments. His own Romantic tastes come out strikingly in the following letter to Stonehewer, June, 1760. "I have received another Scotch packet with a third specimen, inferior in kind . . . but yet full of nature and noble wild feeling. . . . The idea, that struck and surprised me most, is the following. One of them (describing a storm of wind and rain) says: —

> 'Ghosts ride on the tempest to-night;
> Sweet is their voice between the gusts of wind;
> *Their songs are of other worlds!*'

Did you never observe (*while rocking winds are piping loud*) that pause, as the gust is recollecting itself, and rising upon the ear in a shrill and plaintive note, like the swell of an Aeolian

---

[1] Gosse says in his *Life of Gray*, page 163, that Gray not only takes precedence of English poets in the revival of Norse mythology, but even of the Scandinavian writers. But this is going too far. Mallet, in his *Histoire de Dannemarck*, Vol. II., page 309, speaks of a book on the "exploits des rois et des héros du Nord" published at Stockholm in 1737.

[2] *Works*, Vol. III., page 45.

harp? I do assure you there is nothing in the world so like the voice of a spirit." [1] Gray continued to correspond with his friends about Ossian, saying that he had "gone mad" about it.[2]

The best way to show the growth toward Romanticism in Gray's poetry is to quote successively short passages from poems representative of all his periods of production. They will explain themselves.

From the *Ode on the Spring*, written 1742 : —

> " To Contemplation's sober eye
>     Such is the race of Man ;
> And they that creep, and they that fly,
>     Shall end where they began.
> Alike the Busy and the Gay
> But flutter thro' life's little day,
>     In fortune's varying colours drest ;
> Brush'd by the hand of rough Mischance,
> Or chill'd by Age, their airy dance
>     They leave, in dust to rest."

From *The Alliance of Education and Government*, written in 1748 : —

> " As sickly Plants betray a niggard earth,
> Whose barren bosom starves her gen'rous birth,
> Nor genial warmth, nor genial juice retains
> Their roots to feed, and fill their verdant veins ;
> And as in climes, where Winter holds his reign,
> The soil, tho' fertile, will not teem in vain,
> Forbids her gems to swell, her shades to rise,
> Nor trusts her blossoms to the churlish skies ;
> So draw Mankind in vain the vital airs,
> Unform'd, unfriended, by those kindly cares,
> That health and vigour to the soul impart,
> Spread the young thought, and warm the opening heart ;
> So fond Instruction " etc.

[1] *Gray's Works*, Vol. III., page 47.
[2] Mr. Gosse has some interesting remarks on Gray and Ossian in his *Life of Gray*, page 149.

From the *Elegy,* 1742–50 :—

> " Now fades the glimmering landscape on the sight,
>     And all the air a solemn stillness holds,
> Save where the beetle wheels his droning flight,
>     And drowsy tinklings lull the distant folds ;
>
> Save that from yonder ivy-mantled tow'r
>     The mopeing owl does to the moon complain
> Of such, as wandering near her secret bow'r,
>     Molest her ancient solitary reign."

From *The Progress of Poesy,* written 1754 :—

> " Woods, that wave o'er Delphi's steep,
> Isles, that crown th' Aegean deep,
> Fields, that cool Ilissus laves,
> Or where Maeander's amber waves
> In lingering Lab'rinths creep,
> How do your tuneful Echos languish,
> Mute, but to the voice of Anguish?
> Where each old poetic Mountain
>     Inspiration breath'd around ;
> Ev'ry shade and hallow'd Fountain
>     Murmur'd deep a solemn sound ;
> Till the sad Nine in Greece's evil hour
>     Left their Parnassus for the Latian plains.
> Alike they scorn the pomp of tyrant-Power,
>     And coward Vice, that revels in her chains.
> When Latium had her lofty spirit lost,
> They sought, oh Albion ! next thy sea-encircled coast."

From *The Bard,* written 1754–7 :—

> On a rock, whose haughty brow,
>     Frowns o'er old Conway's foaming flood,
> Robed in the sable garb of woe,
>     With haggard eyes the Poet stood ;
> (Loose his beard, and hoary hair
> Streamed, like a meteor; to the troubled air)
> And with a Master's hand, and Prophet's fire,
> Struck the deep sorrows of his lyre.

Hark, how each giant-oak, and desert cave,
    Sighs to the torrent's aweful voice beneath !
O'er thee, oh King ! their hundred arms they wave,
    Revenge on thee in hoarser murmurs breath ;
Vocal no more, since Cambria's fatal day,
To high-born Hoel's harp, or soft Llewellyn's lay."

From *The Fatal Sisters*, written 1761 : —

    " Now the storm begins to lower
        (Haste, the loom of Hell prepare),
    Iron-sleet of arrowy shower
        Hurtles in the darken'd air.

      *      *      *      *

    See the griesly texture grow,
        ('Tis of human entrails made,)
    And the weights, that play below,
        Each a gasping Warriour's head.

      *      *      *      *

    *Mista* black, terrific maid,
        *Sangrida*, and *Hilda* see,
    Join the wayward work to aid ;
        'Tis the woof of victory.

    Ere the ruddy sun be set,
        Pikes must shiver, javelins sing,
    Blade with clattering buckler meet,
        Hauberk crash, and helmet ring."

From *The Descent of Odin*, written 1761 : —

    " In the caverns of the west,
    By *Odin's* fierce embrace comprest,
    A wond'rous Boy shall *Rinda* bear,
    Who ne'er shall comb his raven-hair,
    Nor wash his visage in the stream,
    Nor see the sun's departing beam ;
    Till he on *Hoder's* corse shall smile
    Flaming on the fun'ral pile.
    Now my weary lips I close :
    Leave me, leave me to repose."

The significance of the above quotations is apparent at a glance. *The Descent of Odin* is about as different from the *Ode on the Spring* as can well be imagined.

As he advanced in life, Gray's ideas of poetry grew free in theory as well as in practise. His *Observations on English Metre*, written probably in 1760–61, and published in 1814, contains much interesting matter. Gray had planned to write a History of English poetry, but when he heard that Thomas Warton was engaged in that work, he gave up the idea, and handed over his material and general scheme to Warton. If Gray had completed a history of this kind, it would certainly have been more accurate than Warton's, and would probably have done as much service to Romanticism. A few words may be quoted from the *Observations*, to show how far Gray had advanced in his ideas since 1740. Speaking of Milton, he says, "The more we attend to the composition of Milton's harmony, the more we shall be sensible how he loved to vary his pauses, his measures and his feet, which gives that enchanting air of freedom and wildness to his versification, unconfined by any rules but those which his own feeling and the nature of his subject demands."[1]

Gray's prose remains are deeply interesting to the student of Romanticism. He was one of the first men in Europe who had any real appreciation of wild and Romantic scenery. It has now become so fashionable to be fond of mountains, and lakes, and picturesque landscapes, that it seems difficult to believe that all this is a modern taste. To-day the average summer traveler speaks enthusiastically of precipices, mountain cascades and shaded glens, and even to some extent interprets them by the imagination; but the average eighteenth century sojourner neither could nor would do anything of the sort. This appreciation of the picturesque in external nature has a close kinship with the Romantic movement in literature; for the same emotions are at the foundation of each.

---

[1] *Works*, Vol. I., page 332.

The Classicists had no more love for wild nature than they had for Gothic architecture or Romantic poetry. Let us take Addison as a conspicuous example. "In one of his letters, dated December, 1701, he wrote that he had reached Geneva after 'a very troublesome journey over the Alps. My head is still giddy with mountains and precipices; and you can't imagine how much I am pleased with the sight of a plain!' This little phrase is a good illustration of the contempt for mountains, of the way they were regarded as wild, barbaric, useless excrescences. . . . The love of mountains is something really of modern, very modern, growth, the first traces of which we shall come across towards the middle of the last century. Before that time we find mountains spoken of in terms of the severest reprobation."[1]

Mountains and wild scenery were considered as objects not of beauty or grandeur, but of horror. But in Gray's letters we hear the modern tone.

In this respect he was even more in advance of his contemporaries than in his Romantic poetry. From first to last he was always a lover of wild nature; and, as this taste was so unfashionable, we may be sure of his sincerity. Toward the close of his life, this feeling in Gray becomes more and more noticeable. His Lake Journal is a marvel when we consider its date, for it is written in the true spirit of Wordsworth. But his *early* letters and journals show that he knew how to appreciate Romantic scenery. Take two extracts from his *Journal in France* (1739).[2] These words are interesting simply as showing what attracted Gray's attention: "Beautiful way,

[1] *Perry's Eighteenth Century Literature*, page 145. But much of our modern love for mountains and precipices is doubtless due to the circumstances in which we view them. Carried to the top of the Rigi in a comfortable car, we are in a condition to enjoy to the utmost the glorious view; but if the Rigi represented an obstacle, something that must be passed over with infinite discomfort and even peril, in order to reach a destination on the other side, I am sure we should not appreciate the view so keenly. This was the attitude in which Addison looked at the Alps.

[2] This was printed for the first time by Mr. Gosse in Vol. I. of his edition of *Gray's Works*.

commonly on the side of a hill, cover'd with woods, the river Marne winding in the vale below, and Côteaux, cover'd with vines, riseing gently on the other side ; fine prospect of the town of Joinville, with the castle on the top of the mountain, overlooking it. . . . Ruins of an old castle on the brow of a mountain, whose sides are cover'd with woods." [1] Again, describing the journey to Geneva : " The road runs over a Mountain, which gives you the first tast of the Alps, in it's magnificent rudeness, and steep precipices ; set out from Echelles on horseback, to see the Grande Chartreuse, the way to it up a vast mountain, in many places the road not 2 yards broad ; on one side the rock hanging over you, & on the other side a monstrous precipice. In the bottom runs a torrent . . . that works its way among the rocks with a mighty noise, and frequent Falls. You here meet with all the beauties so savage and horrid [2] a place can present you with ; Rocks of various and uncouth figures, cascades pouring down from an immense height out of hanging Groves of Pine-Trees, & the solemn Sound of the Stream, that roars below, all concur to form one of the most poetical scenes imaginable." [3]

All this is remarkable language for the year 1739. Probably very few private journals of the eighteenth century can show anything similar to it ; for Gray's feelings were, at that time, almost exclusively his own. One more remark of his on Alpine scenery may be quoted. He wrote to Richard West, November 16, 1739 : " I own I have not, as yet, anywhere met with those grand and simple works of Art, that are to amaze one, and whose sight one is to be the better for ; but those of Nature have astonished me beyond expression. In our little journey up to the Grande Chartreuse, I do not remember to have gone ten paces without an exclamation, that there was no restrain-

---

[1] *Works*, Vol. I., page 240.

[2] The word sounds conventional, more like Augustan style ; but what Gray goes on to say shows that it appealed to his own feelings in a very different way.

[3] *Works*, Vol. I., page 244.

ing. Not a precipice, not a torrent, not a cliff, but is pregnant
with religion and poetry. There are certain scenes that would
awe an atheist into belief, without the help of other argument.
One need not have a very fantastic imagination, to see spirits
there at noonday ; you have Death perpetually before your
eyes, only so far removed, as to compose the mind without
frightening it." [1]

Just thirty years later, Gray wrote another journal, which
shows that he had progressed as rapidly in his appreciation of
Nature as he had in his love of wild and passionate poetry.
This is the *Journal in the Lakes*, written in 1769, and published
in 1775. This document is of great value, as throwing light
on the purely imaginative side of Gray's nature. He took this
Lake trip alone, and wrote the Journal simply to amuse his
friend, Dr. Wharton. Here we have a very different view of
nature from that given by Dyer, Thomson and even by the
Wartons. This remarkable Journal is written in the true
Wordsworthian spirit. Gray not only observes but spiritually
interprets nature. Two quotations will suffice to show how
far Gray's taste had advanced since 1739 : " Behind you are
the magnificent heights of *Walla-crag;* opposite lie the thick
hanging woods of Lord Egremont, and *Newland* valley, with
green and smiling fields embosomed in the dark cliffs ; to the
left the jaws of *Borrodale*, with that turbulent chaos of
mountain behind mountain, rolled in confusion ; beneath you,
and stretching far away to the right, the shining purity of the
*Lake*, just ruffled by the breeze, enough to show it is alive,
reflecting rocks, woods, fields, and inverted tops of mountains." [2]

The following passage is perhaps the most striking thing
Gray ever wrote about nature : " In the evening walked alone
down to the Lake by the side of *Crow-Park* after sun-set and
saw the solemn colouring of night draw on, the last gleam of
sunshine fading away on the hill-tops, the deep serene of the

waters, and the long shadows of the mountains thrown across them, till they nearly touched the hithermost shore. At distance heard the murmur of many water-falls not audible in the day-time. Wished for the Moon, but she was *dark to me and silent, hid in her vacant interlunar cave.*" [1]

Mitford said : "No man was a greater admirer of nature than Mr. Gray, nor admired it with better taste." Perhaps Walpole had partly in mind Gray's superior appreciation of Alpine scenery when he wrote, in 1775: "We rode over the Alps in the same chaise, but Pegasus drew on his side, and a cart-horse on mine." [2] There is something noble and truly beautiful in the way in which Walpole always insisted on his own inferiority to Gray. His attitude in this was never cringing ; it was a pure tribute of admiration, and that, too, from a sensitive man who had been repeatedly snubbed by the very object of his praise.

It is interesting to notice the strange and strong contrast between the shy, reserved temperament of Gray, and the pronounced radicalism of his literary tastes. Had he been a demonstrative and gushing person like Mason, his utterances about mountains and Ossianic poetry would not seem so singular ; but that this secluded scholar, who spent most of his hours over his books in Cambridge and the manuscripts in the British Museum, and who was always slow to speak, should have quietly cultivated tastes so distinctly Romantic — this is a noteworthy fact. It seems to show that the one-man power counts for something in literary developments. Gray influenced the age more than the age influenced him ; he led rather than followed. In addition to all the various forces that we have observed as silently working in the Romantic movement, we must add the direct influence of the courage and genius of Gray.

---

[1] *Works*, Vol. I., page 258.
[2] Letter to Cole, December 10, 1775.

# CHAPTER X.

## GENERAL SUMMARY.

In the preceding pages, I have sketched the growth of Romanticism from its first faint manifestations to its practically complete ascendancy. It is evident that a number of various elements entered into the movement. There was the poetry of external nature, which began with Ramsay, Thomson and Dyer; although this was not necessarily Romantic, it exerted a powerful reactionary influence. There was the Change of Form; the yoke of the couplet was slipped off by the revival of blank verse, and by constant experiments in other metres; all of which pointed not to Rule, but to Freedom. Then came the extraordinary influence of Spenser, and the swarm of imitations of his stanza; many of these were not serious, but they helped to further the study of both Spenser and all Elizabethan poetry. The influence of Milton was also a powerful agency — giving to literature a dreamy, melancholy cast, that harmonized with the Sentimentalism on England and the Continent. Then appeared the revival of mediæval taste, in the rage for Gothic art and the love of chivalry. Language itself was made fresh and strong by the influx of ballad literature, which had had friends all through the century, but which leaped into enormous popularity through Percy's *Reliques.* The final blow to Augustan taste came in the form of substituting for its attenuated, classic mythology, the picturesque, Romantic tales of the gods and heroes of the North. Along with this revival of ancient themes appeared the poems of Ossian, claiming remote antiquity, and exercising a deep, if not formative, influence. Lastly, during the critical twenty years from 1750 to 1770, the greatest living man of letters exerted all his poetic powers in the direction of Romanticism.

The Romantic school was aided not only by the poets and story tellers; it had its critical defenders. A number of serious prose works backed up the movement and inspired its supporters. Hogarth's *Analysis of Beauty* (1753) had, perhaps, little to do with the literary side of Romanticism, but as a contribution to the discussion of real beauty and true art it was certainly influential. Hogarth insisted that true art should avoid Regularity; he also pleaded for copying and studying nature and out-door life. Lowth's lectures on the Sacred Poetry of the Hebrews (1753) encouraged the study of the Old Testament from the purely literary point of view, and opened up anew all the grandeur and imagery of Hebrew poetry. The critical side of his work helped also in forming true ideas on the nature of poetry. His chapter on *Poetic Imagery from the Objects of Nature* must have been especially suggestive in those days. Again, in the next year (1754) appeared Thomas Warton's *Observations on the Faery Queen;* a warm, vigorous defense of mediaeval subject and Romantic treatment. In 1759 Young's *Conjectures on Original Composition* took a radical stand. He declared that the time had come to abandon Classic models; and to turn directly to nature and to the inspiration of native genius. He insisted that genius was greater than any rules, and must be a law unto itself. The spectacle of this aged poet boldly flinging off all shackles and defiantly supporting the new school, must have been in itself an inspiration. But most important of all the critical works that aided the Romantic movement, was Joseph Warton's *Essay on Pope* (1756). It is one of the most significant books of the whole century. This was the first open and serious attack on Pope's position as a poet. The tone of it is extraordinarily modern; much of it might have been written by our critics of to-day. Warton insisted that Pope was a great Wit rather than a great Poet; his poetry was strictly not first-class and must forever prevent him from obtaining a place among the highest names. Warton's book was both destructive and constructive; he successfully assailed Pope's lofty position and completely dethroned him and his school; at the same time he elaborated his own theories as to the nature of true Poetry; — and these theories were, of course, Romantic. Although the second volume of Warton's *Essay* did not appear until nearly thirty years after the first, he had articulated in his initial publication distinct doctrines which have formed the Romantic creed from that day to this. He was one of the few conscious apostles of the new school.

On the whole, however, as has been frequently said in these pages, the English Romantic movement was gradual and largely unconscious; it originated in no distinct antagonism to the Augustans — for some of the most influential Romanticists were profound admirers of Pope and Addison — but rather in an instinctive longing for fresh woods and pastures new. It is a curious fact that the French people, always so fickle, extravagant and violent in political and social affairs, should be on the whole so sober and self-restrained in their creative and critical literature; while the English, whose social history shows remarkable self-control and political foresight, have always exhibited Romantic tendencies in literature and art. For this very reason, the Romantic movement in France was a bitter, desperate fight between a band of young reformers and the national literary instinct; while in England the Romantic movement was simply the heart of the people asserting itself — timidly yet instinctively — against the domination of a critical school. Even the genius of a Pope and a Swift, backed by all the shining talent of Augustan men of letters, failed to hold the English mind in any long bondage. Even at the zenith of their glory, the signs of revolt were plainly visible.

# APPENDIX I.

———◦•◦———

A list of Spenserian imitations published from 1700 to 1775. The dates refer not to the composition, but to the publication.

| | | |
|---|---|---|
| 1706. | PRIOR. | "Ode to the Queen." |
| 1713–1721. | PRIOR (?). | "Colin's Mistakes." |
| | POPE. | "The Alley." |
| 1713. | CROXALL. | "An Original Canto of Spencer's Fairy Queen." |
| 1714. | CROXALL. | "Another Original Canto." |
| 1730 (cir.). | WHITEHEAD. | "Vision of Solomon." |
| | WHITEHEAD. | "Ode to the Honourable Charles Townsend." |
| | WHITEHEAD. | "Ode to the Same." |
| 1736. | THOMPSON. | "Epithalamium." |
| 1736. | CAMBRIDGE. | "Marriage of Frederick." |
| 1736–7. | BOYSE. | "The Olive." |
| 1736–7. | BOYSE. | "Psalm XLII." |
| 1737. | AKENSIDE. | "The Virtuoso." |
| 1739. | G. WEST. | "Abuse of Travelling." |
| 1739. | ANON. | "A New Canto of Spenser's Fairy Queen." |
| 1740. | BOYSE. | "Ode to Marquis of Tavistock." |
| 1741 (cir.). | BOYSE. | "Vision of Patience." |
| 1742. | SHENSTONE. | "The School-Mistress" (incomplete form published 1737). |
| 1742–50. | CAMBRIDGE. | "Archimage." |
| 1742. | R. DODSLEY. | "Pain and Patience." |
| 1743. | ANON. | "Albion's Triumph." |
| 1744 (cir.). | R. DODSLEY. | "Death of Mr. Pope." |
| 1744. | AKENSIDE. | "Ode to Curio." |
| 1746. | BLACKLOCK. | "Hymn to Divine Love." |
| | BLACKLOCK. | "Philantheus." |

| 1747. | MASON. "Stanzas in Musaeus." |
| 1747. | RIDLEY. "Psyche." |
| 1747. | LOWTH. "Choice of Hercules." |
| 1747. | UPTON. "A New Canto of Spencer's Fairy Queen." |
| 1747. | BEDINGFIELD. "Education of Achilles." |
|  | PITT. "The Jordan." |
| 1748. | T. WARTON, SR. "Philander." |
| 1748. | THOMSON. "Castle of Indolence." |
| 1749. | POTTER. "A Farewell Hymne to the Country." |
| 1750. | T. WARTON. "Morning." |
| 1751. | G. WEST. "Education." |
| 1751. | T. WARTON. "Elegy on the Death of Prince Frederick." |
| 1751. | MENDEZ. "The Seasons." |
| 1751. | LLOYD. "Progress of Envy." |
| 1751. | AKENSIDE. "Ode." |
| 1751. | SMITH. "Thales." |
| 1753. | T. WARTON. "A Pastoral in the Manner of Spenser." |
| 1754. | DENTON. "Immortality." |
| 1755. | ARNOLD. "The Mirror." |
| 1748–58. | MENDEZ. "Squire of Dames." |
| 1756. | SMART. "Hymn to the Supreme Being." |
| 1757. | THOMPSON. "The Nativity." |
| 1757. | THOMPSON. "Hymn to May." |
| 1758. | AKENSIDE. "To Country Gentlemen of England." |
| 1759. | WILKIE. "A Dream." |
|  | Poem in *Ralph's Miscellany*. |
| 1762. | DENTON. "House of Superstition." |
| 1767. | MICKLE. "The Concubine." |
| 1768. | DOWNMAN. "Land of the Muses." |
| 1771–4. | BEATTIE. "The Minstrel." |
| 1775. | ANON. "Land of Liberty." |
| 1775. | MICKLE. "Stanzas from Introduction to Lusiad." |

# APPENDIX II.

———•◦•———

## THE BALLAD OF WILLIAM AND MARGARET.

David Mallet's literary reputation is chiefly due to a piece of poetry which he never wrote. *William and Margaret* was one of the most popular ballads of the eighteenth century. It appeared in nearly all the numerous miscellanies, both poetic and musical; it was read, sung, and recited on all sides. It was even parodied. With the exception of a few skeptical and unimportant personages, its authorship was universally attributed to Mallet, and men like James Thomson, Dr. Johnson, and Bishop Percy gave him the weight of their authority. The ballad floated all the rest of Mallet's literary performances, and he died a famous man.

The exact date of Mallet's birth is unknown; but he was born in Scotland in 1700, 1701, or 1702. His original name was Malloch, which he changed to Mallet somewhere about the year 1728, and not on his first arrival in London, as is often stated. He came to the metropolis in 1723, as private tutor in the family of the Duke of Montrose. It was not long before he became a man of considerable influence, for it was owing to his timely assistance that Thomson was able to get his *Winter* before the public. This is the only thing for which posterity has reason to be grateful to Mallet; his own writings are mainly dull.

As has been said, it was *William and Margaret* that established Mallet's literary reputation; and it is only within a few years that his claim to its authorship has been successfully assailed. We shall see unfolded one of the prettiest cases of literary forgery on record, as well as one of the meanest, for it took a great deal of deliberate lying on Mallet's part to make good his claim.

The best accounts of this ballad are given by Mr. Frederick Dinsdale, in his edition of the *Ballads and Songs* of Mallet (London, 1857), and by Mr. William Chappell, in his Appendix to the third

volume of the *Roxburghe Ballads* (London, 1880).    Mr. Dinsdale
aggressively believed that Mallet wrote the ballad, but he did not
possess the later and more damaging evidence.    Mr. Chappell proves
that Mallet stole the ballad, but his own account contains inaccuracies
and omits some important facts.

The whole story is as follows : *William and Margaret* first
attracted public attention in a periodical called *The Plain Dealer*,
under date of July 24, 1724.    Aaron Hill, the editor, added the
following note to the poem : —

"I am never more delighted than when I meet with an opportunity to
unveil obscure merit, and produce it into notice. . . .    My having taken
up, in a late perambulation, as I stood upon the top of Primrose Hill, a
torn leaf of one of those Halfpenny Miscellanies which are published for
the use and pleasure of our nymphs of low degree, and known by the name
of *Garlands*, . . . I fell unexpectedly upon a work, for so I have no scruple
to call it, which deserves to live forever ! and which (notwithstanding its
disguise of coarse brown paper, almost unintelligible corruptions of the
sense from the blunders of the press, with here and there an obsolete low
phrase which I have altered for the clearer explanation of the author's
meaning) is so powerfully filled throughout with that blood-curdling, chill-
ing influence of Nature working on our passions (which Criticks call the
sublime) that I have never met it stronger in Homer himself ; nor even in
that prodigious English genius, who has made the Greek our countryman.
The simple title of this piece was, *William and Margaret. A Ballad.* I
am sorry that I am not able to acquaint my Reader with his name to whom
we owe this melancholy piece of finished Poetry ; under the humble title
of a Ballad."

Thus the poem first reached the public attention dressed out with
Hill's "improvements," which practically destroyed its beauty and
strength.    They were all made after the pattern of Augustan taste.

The next we hear of the ballad is in *The Plain Dealer* for
August 28 of the same year (1724).    Hill writes that the poem which
he had published on July 24, he had supposed to be the work of
some old poet long since dead, but that he had been "agreeably
undeceived ; the author of it is alive, and a North Briton."    At the
same time Hill printed a letter which he had received from the
avowed author (Mallet), though he did not as yet mention Mallet's
name.    This letter expressed the pleasure the writer felt in having

his "simple tale" published with so favorable a comment, and gave a detailed and minute account of the circumstances which he said inspired him to write the ballad. He wrote out a pathetic story of a young girl who had been ruined and then deserted by her lover, in consequence of which she died. Mallet said that while meditating on this melancholy event, a scene from the play of the *Knight of the Burning Pestle* entered his mind; especially the lines repeated by old Merrythought, —

> "When it was grown to dark midnight,
>     And all were fast asleep,
> In came Margaret's grimly ghost,
>     And stood at William's feet."

Mallet said this stanza was probably a part of some old ballad, all the rest of which was lost; but these lines coming to him while thinking of the sad story of the dead girl, inspired him to write his own ballad, *William and Margaret*. Along with this letter, Mallet sent his own version of the ballad, which was the one Hill had found and emended. Hill printed the letter, but refused to publish Mallet's copy of the ballad, as he said the sense of the two versions was the same.

All this important matter about Mallet's letter and Hill's August number of *The Plain Dealer*, Mr. Chappell makes no mention of. He must have been ignorant of it, for he says that Mallet *afterward* claimed that he had founded his ballad on the stanza from the old drama; and Mr. Chappell adds very weakly, that Mallet can hardly be supposed to have read Beaumont and Fletcher as early as 1724, because they would not have been included in the curriculum of a University education! This argument tries to prove too much; instead of making Mallet a blacker villain, it only weakens the case against him; because we know that Mallet had read the play by 1724, and there is evidence to show that the best English authors were at that time very widely read and imitated in Scotland. Although Mallet did steal the ballad, there is no reason why we should not give the devil his due.

To resume; the only copy of *William and Margaret* before the public thus far was Hill's mangled version published in July, 1724. Mr. Chappell says that its next appearance was in Allan Ramsay's

*Tea-Table Miscellany*, published the same year. It is true that the ballad did appear in Vol. II. of this *Miscellany*, in Mallet's own version, and signed " D. M." But *when* Vol. II was first published, is not so certain. There is good reason for assigning its date to 1725 or 1726, rather than to 1724. If we only knew exactly when the volume was published, it might be of great service in tracing the history of this ballad.

In 1725, *William and Margaret* appeared in Vol. III of the *Collection of Old Ballads*. This version is neither Aaron Hill's nor the one published by Mallet. According to Mr. Chappell, it must be a reprint from the original ballad published before the *Knight of the Burning Pestle*. But as this copy in *Old Ballads* differs from Mallet's version only in slight verbal changes, its publication would not have excited much suspicion.

By 1726, at any rate, Mallet had the credit of authorship, for Thomson, in the Preface to the second edition of *Winter*, alludes to him as the composer of *William and Margaret*. In 1728 Mallet published the ballad under his own name, along with his poem, *The Excursion*, and in successive editions of Mallet's works it regularly appeared.

The proof of the forgery did not come till the year 1878, when a black-letter copy of the old ballad of *William and Margaret* was brought to light. This copy bears a Queen Anne stamp, and *on this stamp* rests the evidence against Mallet. In 1711–12 an act of Parliament was passed requiring stamps upon newspapers. This Act was not meant to apply to ballads, and, as Mr. Chappell says, "they were speedily excepted from its operation." This ballad is exactly the same as the one published in Mallet's works, with the exception of a few verbal alterations. It could not have been written by Mallet, for he would have been more than a marvel of precocity to produce such a thing at the age of eleven or twelve years. This Queen Anne stamp completely disposes of Mallet's claim ; and thus it is altogether probable that *William and Margaret*, as it stands, is one of the old English ballads, and not an eighteenth century production at all.

In a case like this, where we know for certain only a part of the facts, we naturally ask, How did Mallet's name come to be so firmly joined to this ballad as to hold the credit of its authorship for 150 years ? This is largely a matter of conjecture ; but as everybody in possession of the facts has a right to amuse himself in constructing a theory, it may not be out of place to suggest the following explanation.

We know that Hill published his disfigured version in July, 1724. Mallet saw it in print and noticed that no one claimed its authorship. Having the true copy in his own possession, he made a radical change in the first line, with trifling verbal alterations in the other stanzas, trumped up a story of the circumstances that led him to compose the poem and sent both story and poem to *The Plain Dealer*, taking care to withhold his name from the public. With great cunning he himself quoted the passage from the old drama, thus forestalling future criticisms on that score. Hill published Mallet's unsigned letter, but refused to publish the enclosed version of the ballad, probably because he liked his own improvements too well to have them superseded. Then Mallet, wanting a publisher for his own copy, handed it over to Allan Ramsay — who was thoroughly unscrupulous in matters of authorship — and it appeared in Vol. II of the *Tea-Table Miscellany*, signed "D. M." As no one put up a counter-claim to Mallet, he grew bolder, and in 1728 published the ballad with his full name in a volume of his own verse. Such seems to be a natural and probable account of what he did, why he did it, and what the results of his action were.

Mallet never wrote anything in his life that can compare with this ballad, and he never attempted anything in the same manner and verse-form until 1760, five years before his death. He then published an original ballad in the same metre, called *Edwin and Emma*. No one has ever considered it worth while to dispute his claim to this poem. It is indeed a silly piece of verse. Perhaps he thought matters would look less suspicious if he had more than one ballad to show for his work. But, unhappily for his reputation, *Edwin and Emma* is like *William and Margaret* only in structure. It is a ridiculous composition, highly artificial in sentiment and in language. It has none of the spirit of the former ballad. A few stanzas quoted from each will make further comment unnecessary. *William and Margaret* begins as follows : —

> " When all was wrapt in dark Midnight
> And all were fast asleep,
> In glided Margaret's grimly ghost,
> And stood at William's feet.

> " Her face was like the April morn,
>     Clad in a wintry cloud,
> And clay-cold was her lily hand,
>     That held the sable shroud.
>
> " So shall the fairest face appear
>     When Youth and Years are flown ;
> Such is the robe that Kings must wear
>     When Death has reft their crown."

Compare this with a passage taken from *Edwin and Emma :* —

> " Long had she filled each youth with love,
>     Each maiden with despair ;
> And though by all a wonder owned,
>     Yet knew not she was fair.
>
> " Till Edwin came, the pride of swains,
>     A soul devoid of art ;
> And from whose eye, serenely mild,
>     Shone forth the feeling heart.
>
> " A mutual flame was quickly caught ;
>     Was quickly too revealed ;
> For neither bosom lodged a wish,
>     That virtue keeps concealed."

*William and Margaret* has an importance, independent of its
authorship, as contributing to the early hidden growth of the English
Romantic movement.   Its great popularity in " the age of prose and
reason " shows that there was a love for poetry of this kind, however
much fashion condemned it in the abstract.   For its introduction to
the public, we must be grateful to Aaron Hill — a pompous, short-
sighted person — and Allan Ramsay — a sturdy, unscrupulous, half-
vulgar fellow.   They builded better than they knew.

# INDEX.

---

This book may be kept
# FOURTEEN DAYS
A fine of 2 cents will be charged for each day
the book is kept overtime.

| | | | |
|---|---|---|---|
| Apr 18 '33 | Oct 16 '39 | pd | |
| May 12 '33 | Nov 2 '39 | 17 Mar '48 | |
| May 27 '33 | Apr 12 '40 | | |
| May 2 '34 HE | Apr 26 '4 R | | |
| May 28 '34 H U | Jul 23 | pd | |
| Jul 14 '34 H U | Sep 30 '4 | | |
| Apr 8 '35 PE | RESERVE | | |
| Jan 28 '36 T | Sep 21 '40 | | |
| Jul 3 '36 T | Apr 7 '41 | | |
| Mar 5 '37 HE | RESERVE | | |
| Mar 24 '37 E | Sep 20 '41 | | |
| Apr 23 '37 | RESERVE | | |
| May 7 '37 | Sep 15 '42 | | |
| Mar 19 '38 | 23 Mar 4 45 | | |
| Mar 29 '38 | ON RESERVE | | |
| May 17 '38 | 17 | | |
| May 25 '38 | RESERVE | | |
| Aug 2 '39 E | Sep 194 | | |